The Club of Hercules

The Club of Hercules

Studies in the Classical Background of Paradise Lost

Davis P. Harding

ILLINOIS STUDIES IN LANGUAGE AND LITERATURE: *Vol. 50*

THE UNIVERSITY OF ILLINOIS PRESS
URBANA, 1962

For my Mother and Father

Preface

Unless he is imperious, every poet writes mainly with a particular audience in mind — his own, the contemporary one. He tries to give his readers what he thinks they want or at least what he knows they will understand, if the presentation is made adequate. Milton could reasonably suppose in his "fit audience" a more or less intimate knowledge of two vast areas of learning, the Bible and the classical languages and literature, especially Latin. That presupposition is clearly not valid today. Educational patterns have drastically changed. The Bible is out of the schools and back within the almost exclusive jurisdiction of the churches; it is reverenced, as it should be, but it is not pondered and studied in the sense that it was pondered and studied by lay men and women in Milton's century. For a poem like *Paradise Lost,* the deprivation must be accounted immeasurable. So it has been, too, with classical literature. When colleges and universities decided to abandon Latin and Greek as prerequisites for admission, the die was cast. There are few responsible teachers who have not been frustrated by the experience of trying to communicate something of the power and glory of *Paradise Lost* to a generation of students who have had at best small Latin and at worst no Greek at all. It is primarily for these students, a blameless majority, that this book has been written: hence the method of quotation from classical authors and indeed the shape and character of the whole work. Documentation for the same reason has been kept to an essential minimum.

There is, of course, no genuine substitute for a firsthand knowledge of Latin and Greek literature. In the following pages I have merely attempted to suggest, not rigidly to define, some of the ways in which Milton has turned that literature to account at every level of the poem's meaning — plot, structure, characterization, and pre-eminently style. The thesis is simple. We cannot, with justice, ignore the relations of *Paradise Lost* to the tradition which has provided so much of its vitality and grandeur.

These studies were begun under the auspices of the Guggenheim Foundation, for whose substantial aid I am deeply grateful. I should also like to thank the University of Illinois Press, and the editors of the *Journal of English and Germanic Philology*, for permission to reprint the short essay entitled "Milton's Bee-Simile" which appeared recently in *Milton Studies in Honor of Harris Francis Fletcher* (1961). To the assistant editor of that press, Mrs. Elizabeth G. Dulany, who had the unenviable task of seeing this volume through the press, I here pay apologetic tribute.

To Professor Douglas Bush of Harvard, Professor Charles Osgood of Princeton, and Professor and Mrs. Marvin T. Herrick of the University of Illinois I owe a continuing debt of gratitude which it is once again a pleasure to acknowledge. I am also under obligation to the following friends and colleagues at Yale University who, in one way or another, contributed significantly to this study: Professors Edmund T. Silk, Benjamin C. Nangle, the late Stanley T. Williams, and A. Dwight Culler. Above all, I must thank Professor Harris Fletcher, who may regret it now but who first taught me to love Milton.

Contents

All he said, was, I now believe, right, but he should have taken me away from school. He would have taught me nothing but Greek and Latin, and I would now be an educated man, and would not have to look in useless longing at books that have been through the poor mechanism of translation, the builders of my soul, nor face authority with the timidity born of excuse and evasion.

WILLIAM BUTLER YEATS

CHAPTER ONE

Fit Audience

Responsible critics have always recognized that a tradition can be extraordinarily useful to a poet who anticipates its dangers and circumvents them. A tradition is a birthright, renounced at the poet's imminent peril, enabling him to profit from the experiments of others, to build upon their strong foundations. It puts at his disposition a rich inheritance of aesthetic devices and techniques which experience has proved of value. By using them, the traditional poet is able to achieve clarity in plan and economy in execution. His art, therefore, is principally an evocative art; that is, he extends and enriches his meanings by a strategy of deliberate allusiveness to the poetry of the past.

The allusion is a protean device, and may appear now in one guise, now in another, ranging all the way from the borrowed incident or the direct quotation to the subtlest variations on old words, cadences, or rhythms. But in whatever shape it appears, with the good poet its purpose is seldom merely decorative. By means of it, he is able to convey to the reader an idea or an emotion which he could not convey in any other fashion without some kind of loss.

These are powerful advantages and, by securing them, the poet does well. No more than the man in the street can he afford to ignore the experience of the past. But human experience is not static. Just as it is a sign of social irresponsibility in an individual to live by the past alone, so it is a sign of aesthetic irresponsibility on the part of the poet. The responsible poet never leaves a tradition precisely as he found it. He makes it conform both to his own individual experience and the assimilated experience of the age in which he lives. In a word, he re-creates the tradition; he makes it live again. To estimate the degree of his success in revitalizing the poetry of the past would therefore appear to be one way — and perhaps for this kind of poet the most fruitful way — of measuring his achievement.

Paradise Lost is an epic poem conceived and written in the classical tradition. Now it is obvious that the usefulness of a tradition must depend to a marked extent upon its strength and vitality. The more

1

widespread and deeply a poet may assume his readers to have shared his literary and cultural experience, the greater his opportunities, it would seem, for subtle and original treatment. Milton wrote in the classical tradition because he believed that he could write a finer poem by cleaving to it. But he also knew that he had an audience thoroughly qualified to understand the kind of poem he was obliged to write.

Long before Milton began writing *Paradise Lost*, educated men had been living what Christopher Dawson has called a "double life." Physically confined to their own world, intellectually and imaginatively they lived in the world of Greece and Rome. "The classical world," Dawson writes, "was the standard of their thought and conduct. In a sense, it was more real to them than their own world, for they had been taught to know the history of Rome better than that of England or modern Europe; to judge their literature by the standard of Quintilian, and to model their thought on Cicero and Seneca. Ancient history was history in the absolute sense, and the ages that followed were a shadowy and unreal world which could only be rationalized by being related in some way to the classical past." [1] Cut off from a true appreciation of his own native literary past by the linguistic barrier, unwilling out of patriotism to create a new literature wholly upon Italian and French models, and fearful of innovation, the typical English Renaissance poet found it all the easier to justify in his own mind the conviction, drilled into him from his school days, that the surest path to successful achievement in poetry was "to follow the ancients."

Today we know more about those school days and are consequently in a better position to gauge their influence on the reading and listening habits of Renaissance Englishmen. The first thing to notice is the narrow scope of the studies. From the time a boy entered grammar school, which was normally at the age of seven, to the time he departed for trade or university some seven or eight years later, he was exposed to nothing but the classical languages and literatures. In fact, once the schoolboy had mastered the rudiments of Latin grammar and such handbooks of conversational Latin as the popular *Sententiae Pueriles* and the *Colloquia* of Erasmus or Corderius, he was even expected (and often required by school statute) to converse in Latin while he remained within the precincts of the school, or at least at meals and in the classroom. No provision was made for the study of such "modern" subjects as English literature or European

---

[1] "Edward Gibbon," *Proceedings of the British Academy*, XX (1934), 6–7.

history or mathematics or science. Here, for example, is a list of authors we have every reason to believe were taught at St. Paul's when Milton was there as a pupil: Cato (*Disticha Moralia*), Aesop (*Fabulae*), Erasmus (*Colloquia*), the comedies of Terence, Ovid (*De Tristibus* and the *Metamorphoses*), Caesar, the historians Justin and Sallust, Virgil, Cicero, Horace, the minor Greek poets, Homer, Euripides, Isocrates, Persius, and Juvenal.[2]

In providing so much instruction in Greek, St. Paul's was exceptional. Although Greek had established itself in school curricula by 1600,[3] only a very few schools had penetrated beyond the reading of the New Testament and Nowell's Catechism to a study of the major Greek authors, probably because of a shortage of qualified teachers. This is important. It clearly means that Renaissance poets could not safely presuppose in their average readers a close verbal knowledge of Greek literature. There is interesting confirmation of this fact from Milton himself. In a letter to Alexander Gill, dated December 4, 1634, he confesses to his friend and erstwhile teacher that a Greek ode he had written the week before was "the first and only thing" he had composed in that language since he had left St. Paul's. He employs himself instead, he says, in Latin and English, for whoever spends his time on poems written in Greek "runs a risk of singing mostly to the deaf." [4]

The central aim of the grammar schools remained the same as it had been in the Middle Ages: that is, to teach the reading, writing, and speaking of Latin. But in the meantime the invention of printing by movable type had worked momentous changes. Because of the scarcity of manuscripts, the medieval schoolmaster had been obliged to rely mainly on the methods of oral instruction. The invention of

[2] The earliest known curriculum of St. Paul's School was found among the papers of Thomas Gale, who was High Master from 1672 to 1697. Its contents have been extensively analyzed by T. W. Baldwin, *William Shakspere's Small Latine & Lesse Greeke* (Urbana, Ill., 1944), I, 118–33, and by Donald L. Clark, *John Milton at St. Paul's School* (New York, 1948), pp. 109–26. The latter prints a transcript of the manuscript. Both Baldwin and Clark are of the opinion that the Gale manuscript provides, with perhaps a few exceptions, the curriculum Milton followed at St. Paul's. Unfortunately, this manuscript usually does not supply the titles of the works studied. I base my list of authors on the curriculum as Clark has reconstructed it (p. 121).

[3] For a list of grammar schools whose statutes enjoined the study of Greek up to the year 1600, see Foster Watson, *The English Grammar Schools to 1660* (Cambridge, Eng., 1908), pp. 491–93. Watson concludes: "Greek may be said to have established itself in the Grammar Schools after this date [1600]."

[4] *Complete Works of John Milton*, edited by various hands under the general directorship of F. A. Patterson (18 vols., New York, 1931–38), XII, 17. Henceforth all references to Milton's prose will be to this edition, cited as *Works*.

printing, by flooding the schools with Latin texts and miscellaneous "helps to learning," not only established easier channels of communication between the master and his pupils, but encouraged a new pedagogical method, based on a closer attention to detail and the increased use of written exercises. Furthermore, at the same time that the humanists were entering their strongest pleas for a "clene and chast Latin," the invention of printing had made available to the humblest schoolmaster the whole new and exciting corpus of classical apparatus and scholarship.

It is small wonder, under such circumstances, that protests against the "barbarisms" of medieval Latin should mount and that, as a corrective, educators should recommend the careful study and close imitation of the purest and most elegant of the Latin authors. "The essential change in school teaching of Latin in the Renascence spirit from the Mediaeval period," writes Foster Watson, "is the emphasis on the reproduction of accuracy in the imitation of classical Latin." [5] Style and the problems of style became a major preoccupation of the schools.

Whatever its defects, no one who has studied the Renaissance grammar-school system would be likely to concede that there has ever been a time when students were encouraged to read prose and poetry quite as closely. But on so important a point it will be better not to generalize. In the reconstruction of pedagogical methods and practices during the first half of the seventeenth century, three contemporary books have proved especially helpful. The first of these is John Brinsley's *Ludus Literarius*, which had a first edition in 1612 and another in 1627; the second is the same author's *A Consolation for Our Grammar Schooles*, published in 1622; and the third is Charles Hoole's *A New Discovery of the Old Art of Teaching Schoole*, published in 1660, but written, as the author tells us on the title page, twenty-three years earlier. Both Brinsley and Hoole were practicing schoolmasters, and both assure their readers, on numerous occasions, that their methods and aims differ, where they differ at all, only in details from those practiced in the better grammar schools of the nation. [6]

---

[5] Watson, p. 306.

[6] For instance, Hoole writes: "In the mean time you may observe that *the Method* which I have here discovered, *is* for the most part contrived *according to what* is commonly *practised* in England and foreign countries. . . . *The* subject *matter* which *is* taught, is the same with that which is generally used by *Grammars, Authours, and Exercises. . . . " A New Discovery of the Old Art of Teaching Schoole*, ed. E. T. Campagnac (Liverpool and London, 1913), pp. 204–5.

Their systems reflect, on almost every page, the prevalent conviction that the surest way for a schoolboy to achieve elegance in spoken and written Latin was to imitate the purest Roman authors, or, as Brinsley puts it:

In this matter of versifying, as in all the former exercises, I take this Imitation of the most excellent patternes, to be the surest rule, both for phrase and whatsoever: And therefore I would have the chiefest labor to make these purest Authors our owne, as *Tully* for prose, so *Ovid* and *Virgil* for verse, so to speake and write in Latine for the phrase, as they did.[7]

Imitation in this sense was conceived of as a twofold process: the first step was to "analyze" the model in order to ascertain its virtues and the artistic principles underlying them. The second step was to apply these principles in a direct imitation of the model.[8] I shall not at this time discuss the practicality of this approach to teaching boys of grammar-school age the technique of versification. It will be enough for the present to note that the method, especially as applied to authors writing in an unfamiliar tongue, could not fail to discourage any tendency toward glib and facile reading habits.

But let us return to Brinsley and, since we are concerned primarily with the contemporary reader's response to poetry, to the way in which Brinsley would have his pupils come to the study of the Latin poets.

In Virgil, Horace, and other the chiefe and most approved Schoole Authors in Poetrie and Prose, to resolve any peece, for all these points of learning, and to do it in good Latine:
Construing, to give propriety of words and sense, and also to expound in good phrase.
Scanning the Verses, and giving a reason thereof.
Shewing the difficulties of Grammar.
Observing the Elegáncies of Rhetoricke in Tropes and Figures.
Noting Phrases and Epithets, with other principall observations.
So to reade over so much of the chiefe Latine Poets, as Virgil, Horace etc. and of other the best Authors, as shall be thought necessary, by that time, that by reason of their yeares they be in any measure thought fit, for their

---

[7] *Ludus Literarius: or The Grammar Schoole* (London, 1612), p. 195.

[8] See Charles Butler, *Oratoriae Libri Duo* (London, 1629), quoted by Clark, p. 152. Presumably, although he does not say so, the translation is also Clark's. "Exercise consists in Genesis and Analysis. It is Genesis when we compose our own orations according to the precepts of Art and in imitation of the Orators. It is Analysis when we take apart [*resolvimus*] the orations of others, observing in them what rules of Art are followed and what virtues of the authors are worthy of imitation. It is Imitation when we copy the method [*rationem*] of speaking of another. There are two rules in Imitation: that we should imitate those who are excellent and those qualities in them which are excellent." Although Butler is speaking of oratory, his comments are obviously just as applicable to poetic imitation.

discretion, to go unto the University; and to be able to go thorough the rest of themselves, by ordinary helpes.[9]

Obviously, as Brinsley implies, his pupils could not have attended to all these minutiae and, at the same time, have read extensively in the various school authors. For example, by proceeding at the rate of about six or eight verses per lesson, which is the pace Brinsley recommends, it would be impossible to get very far, in the course of a semester, in a poem of the ample proportions of, say, Ovid's *Metamorphoses*. The object was clearly not to read as much poetry as possible but to learn to read a little of it well. Then, having acquired skill in reading, the students would be better "able to go thorough the rest of themselves, by ordinary helpes." That the intensive method of studying literature was the norm for the period is attested on all sides. It accounts for the constant, unremitting emphasis the schoolmaster was wont to put on review, and it helps explain the importance he ascribed to rote learning.[10]

Not until his students had learned to "resolve" (*resolvere*) — that is, analyze — poetry would Brinsley permit them "to meddle with making a verse." Of the Latin poets, Ovid was considered the easiest to imitate, and hence in Renaissance grammar schools, exercises in poetical imitation generally began with the study of his *Tristia*, followed by the *Metamorphoses*.[11] Since Ovid as a rule was studied either in the third or fourth form or both, this would mean that the average schoolboy was turning out Latin verses by the time he was nine or at the latest ten years old.[12] Thus Hoole would have his pupils begin the writing of Latin verse in the fourth form, as soon as they had mastered "Ovids little book de tristibus." He recommends the following method:

Take a Distick or two, which they know not where to finde, and transpose the words, as different as may be from a verse, and when you have made one to construe them, dismisse them all to their seates, to try who can return them first into true verses, without one anothers suggesting. When

---

[9] *A Consolation for Our Grammar Schooles*, ed. Thomas C. Pollock (New York, 1943), p. 54.

[10] At St. Paul's School, Friday mornings, at least in the lower school (that is, from the first form through the fourth), were entirely given over to "A Repetition of what hath been said the whole weeke." From the transcript of the Gale curriculum reproduced in Clark, pp. 110–13. On the importance ascribed to memory work, see the same author, pp. 168–70. See also below, pp. 7–8.

[11] Baldwin, II, 417 ff.

[12] Consequently, we should not be surprised to learn from John Aubrey, whose source was Christopher Milton, the poet's brother, that Milton had by the age of ten "composed many Copies of verses, which might well become a riper age." *Early Lives of Milton*, ed. Helen Darbishire (London, 1932), p. 10.

they have all dispatched, cause him whom you conceive to be the weakest, to compare what he hath done with his Authour, and to prove his verses by the Rules of *Prosodia.*

You may sometimes set them to varie one and the same verse, by transposing the same words, as many several wayes as they can. Thus this verse may be turned 104. waies.

Est mea spes Christus solus qui de cruce pendet

And sometimes you may cause them to keep the same sense, and alter the words [pp. 159–60].

At this juncture Hoole proudly quotes a distich in John Stockwood's *Progymnasma Scholasticum*, which that author had succeeded in varying four hundred and fifty ways. Such exercises were certain to make Renaissance schoolboys highly word-conscious and thoroughly alive to the possibilities inherent in the artificial ordering of speech.

After Ovid had been mastered came the study and imitation of Virgil, to quote Hoole, "the Prince and purest of all Latine Poets." His three major works — the *Eclogues*, the *Georgics*, and the *Aeneid* — form what might be called the hard core of the Renaissance grammar-school curriculum. Of all the school authors, only Cicero was studied with a comparable intensity. It is probably not too much to say that Renaissance schoolboys practically knew Virgil by heart. This is how Hoole advocates the study of the *Eclogues*, which he would have "constantly and throughly read by this form [the Fifth] on Mondaies and Tuesdaies for after-noon lessons."

They may begin with ten or twelve verses at a lesson in the *Eclogues*, which they may first repeat *memoriter*, as well as they can possibly.

Construe and parse, and scan and prove exactly.

Give the Tropes and Figures with their definitions.

Note out [of] the Phrases and Epithites, and other Elegancies.

Give the Histories or descriptions belonging to the proper Names, and their Etymologies [pp. 178–79].

Renaissance schoolmasters were apparently unanimous in the significance they attached to memorizing prose and poetry and to the recitation of the memorized passages. Rote learning, however, was not an end in itself. By means of it, it was hoped that the cadences and rhythms of the great poets and orators would be impressed upon the inner ear, as it were, of the student with a delicacy and force not otherwise possible. So Hoole:

But for gaining a smooth way of versifying, and to be able to express much matter in few words, and very fully to the life, I conceive it very necessary for Scholars to be very frequent in perusing *Ovid* and *Virgil*, and afterwards such kind of Poets, as they are themselves delighted with all, either for more variety of verse, or the wittinesse of conceit sake. And the Master indeed should cause his Scholars to recite a piece of *Ovid* or *Virgil*, in his hearing now and then, that the very tune of these pleasant verses may be imprinted in their mindes, so that when ever they are put to compose a verse, they make it glide as even as those in their Authours [pp. 187–88].

There was no adequate substitute for the phrase book or common-place book which the schoolboy, and later the grown man, was able to carry about in his head. Another schoolmaster, John Milton himself, was equally impressed with the aesthetic services a good memory could render. As usual, he makes no allowances for the "weaker sort."

Then will the choise Histories, *Heroic Poems*, and *Attic* Tragedies of state-liest and most regal argument, with all the famous Political Orations offer themselves; which if they were not only read; but some of them got by memory, and solemnly pronounc't with right accent, and grace, as might be taught, would endue them even with the spirit and vigor of *Demosthenes* or *Cicero, Euripides* or *Sophocles.*[13]

It was an age, we must remember, when an Erasmus could memorize Terence and Horace before his fourteenth birthday.

No discussion of the reading and listening habits of Renaissance Englishmen can fail to take into account one other highly important school discipline, that of rhetoric. "The high repute of Rhetoric and its important place in the curriculum," Watson testifies, "is perhaps to the modern reader the most striking feature of the school work of the first half of the seventeenth century." [14] As applied to poetry, rhetoric was the study of the multifarious devices poets employed to depart from the normal, everyday patterns of language, "drawing it," in the words of the Elizabethan critic Puttenham, "from plainnesse and simplicitie to a certain doublenesse." [15] These devices were called Tropes and Figures, and, as we saw above, one of the steps in the analysis of a passage of poetry was to "Give the Tropes and Figures with their definitions," presumably much in the manner that E. K. glosses this line from the *Shepheardes Calendar*:

> I love thilke lasse, (alas why doe I love?)

E. K. comments: "a prety Epanorthosis in these two verses, and withall a Paronomasia or playing with the word." [16] Many contemporary textbooks on rhetoric list as many as one hundred and fifty Figures, and the Renaissance schoolboy was expected to know them

---

[13] "Of Education" in *Works*, IV, 285–86.
[14] Watson, pp. 3–4.
[15] *The Arte of English Poesie*, ed. G. D. Willcock and A. Walker (Cambridge, Eng., 1936), p. 154.
[16] *Januarye*, gloss on line 61.

by heart and to be able to define them. Again it seems advisable to quote Hoole, who would begin the study of rhetoric in the fourth form:

> Thus they may have liberty to learn Rhetorick on Mondayes, Tuesdayes, and Wednesdayes, for morning Parts. And to enter them in that Art of fine speaking, they may make use of *Elementa Rhetorices*, lately printed by *Mr. Dugard*, and out of it learn the Tropes and Figures, according to the definitions given by *Talaeus*, and afterwards more illustrated by *Mr. Butler*. . . .

> These *Elementa Rhetorices* in their first going over, should be explained by the Master, and construed by the Scholars, and every example compared with its Definition. And the Scholars should now be diligent of themselves to observe every Trop and Figure, that occurre in their present Authours, and when they say, to render it with its full definition, and if any be more eminent and worthy observation then others, to write it down in their Common-place-book, and by this means they will come to the perfect understanding of them in a quarter of a yeares times, and with more ease commit it all to memory by constant parts, saying a whole Chapter together at once; which afterwards they may keep by constant Repetitions, as they do their Grammar [pp. 132, 133–34].

In many Renaissance textbooks of Latin poetry, the editors identify in marginal annotations the Figures as they appear in the text.

Of course, it does not follow that the schoolboy who had a nose "for smelling out the odoriferous flowers of fancy, the jerks of invention" was for that reason a better reader of poetry. He had to try to see what the Figure did for the poem. Thus, in the following passage from the First Book of *Paradise Lost*, the mere identification by the schoolboy of the Figure contained in the lines as an instance of agnomination would demonstrate little more than ordinary diligence and alertness.

> Next *Chemos*, th'obscene dread of *Moabs* Sons,
> From *Aroar* to *Nebo*, and the wild
> Of Southmost *Abarim*; in *Hesebon*
> And *Horonaim*, *Seons* Realm, beyond
> The flowry Dale of *Sibma* clad with Vines
> And *Eleale* to th'*Asphaltick* Pool.

> 1.406–11

A modern critic has pointed out what it is which helps make these lines so effective. Calling attention to Milton's previous mention of "Abominations" (1.389), "that opprobrious Hill" (1.403), and such place names as *Rabba*, *Argob*, and *Basan* (1.397–98), he observes: "Other emphatic *b*'s and *p*'s appear throughout the passage, *besmeared*, *blood*, *timbrels*, *worshipped*. There is a kind of extenuated pun, a fleeting shadow of a pun, an extension of the ideas of obscen-

ity and abomination through the echo of sounds." [17] The comment is
acute, and it would be an unusual schoolboy indeed who could so
accurately define the reason for the peculiar effectiveness of these
lines. But the better schoolmasters apparently expected him to try.
"The common scholemasters," sarcastically remarks Richard Sherry
in a book on rhetoric which appeared in 1550, "be wont in readynge,
to saye unto their scholers: *Hic est figura*: and sometyme to axe them,
Per quam figuram? But what profit is herein if they go no further?" [18]

No age has produced a poetry richer in brilliant and daring figures
of speech than the Renaissance. To what extent the Renaissance
passion for rhetoric contributed to this richness we can never fully
know. But one thing is certain. The poets of the period would not
have written in such a highly figurative manner unless they knew
they could count on an audience capable of responding to it. In this
connection, Henry Peacham's warning to fledgling orators is illuminating; he is speaking of synecdoche, but his comment is clearly
applicable to all figurative writing or speaking. "The Orator useth
this figure chiefly when he is well perswaded concerning the wise-
dom of his hearers, that they are of sufficient capacitie and understanding to collect his meaning, whereupon he maketh the bolder
to remove his speech from the vulgar maner of speaking to figurative
forme, whereby he giveth it a grace which otherwise it should want,
forcing the understanding of his hearer to a deeper consideration of
the sense and meaning." [19] Whatever else we may say about Milton's
"fit audience, though few" there can be no doubt that it was unusu-
ally well equipped to understand his uses of classical literature and
had, furthermore, developed a background of reading and listening
habits which guaranteed a closer and more intelligent inspection of
Paradise Lost than most modern readers are qualified to give it.

It must be conceded that the Renaissance school system was ideal-
istic in the extreme, and it is easy to find matter for amusement in
Brinsley's naive contention that, if other schoolmasters would follow
his methods, they could have their best pupils "in a short time attaine
to that ripenesse, as that they who know not the places where they
imitate, shall hardly discerne in many verses, whether the verse bee
Virgils verse, or the schollars." [20] Schoolboys are schoolboys, and those

[17] William K. Wimsatt, "Verbal Style Logical and Counterlogical," *PMLA*,
LXV (March, 1950), 11.
[18] From the "Epystle" to his *A Treatise of Schemes and Tropes* (London, 1550).
[19] *The Garden of Eloquence* (London, 1593), p. 18.
[20] *Ludus Literarius*, p. 194.

of the seventeenth century could not have been much different from those of any other time. The Renaissance school system, it is clear, assumed a maturity in the average schoolboy which he could hardly have possessed. We remember Samuel Butler's ironic couplet:

> For all a rhetorician's rules
> Teach nothing but to name his tools [21]

And we remember, too, Milton's famous criticism of that "preposterous exaction, forcing the empty wits of Children to compose Theams, Verses, and Orations, which are the acts of ripest judgment and the final work of a head fill'd by long reading and observing, with elegant maxims, and copious invention." [22] On the other hand, the hard, driving methods of the Renaissance schoolmasters, their devotion to the aims of a humanistic education, their unflagging emphasis on the importance of the word and phrase, and their faith in the techniques of close imitation must inevitably have produced a body of readers whose response to poetry would be more than half-awake, who knew how to construe meaning, and were prepared to make the effort. And, after all, the system did produce, or helped to produce, poets who wrote and published neo-Latin verse of a very high order.

Among these poets was John Milton. A discussion of a short passage from one of the earlier Latin poems may be of some aid in showing his mastery over schoolboy techniques of imitation. I have selected, more or less at random, some typical lines from the *Fifth Elegy*, a poem written in his twentieth year. The elegy as a whole commemorates the universal creativity which comes with spring, and it sees that creativity as stemming, symbolically, from the mythological union of Phoebus and Tellus, the Sun-father and the Earth-mother.

> Cur te, inquit, cursu languentem Phoebe diurno
>   Hesperiis recipit Caerula mater aquis?
> Quid tibi cum Tethy? Quid cum Tartesside lymphâ,
>   Dia quid immundo perluis ora salo?
> Frigora Phoebe meâ melius captabis in umbrâ,
>   Huc ades, ardentes imbue rore comas.
> Mollior egelidâ veniet tibi somnus in herbâ,
>   Huc ades, & gremio lumina pone meo.
> Quáque jaces circum mulcebit lene susurrans
>   Aura per humentes corpora fusa rosas.
> Nec me (crede mihi) terrent Semelëia fata,
>   Nec Phäetonteo fumidus axis equo;

---

[21] *Hudibras*, 1.1.89–90.
[22] "Of Education" in *Works*, IV, 278.

Cum tu Phoebe tuo sapientius uteris igni,
Huc ades & gremio lumina pone meo.
Sic Tellus lasciva suos supirat amores; [23]

El. 5.81–95

"Oh, why! Apollo, must it be the cerulean ocean-mother who receives thee when thou comest to the west weary from thy day's course? What is Tethys to thee? What to thee the Hesperian tide? Why wilt thou bathe thy divine face in impure brine? A better coolness, Apollo, thou mayst find in my shade. Come hither, dip thy hot locks in my dew. A softer sleep shall come to thee in the cool grass. Come hither, and lay thy glories in my breast. Where thou liest a gently whispering breeze will soothe our bodies as we sink relaxed in dewy roses. Believe me, I fear not Semele's fate; I fear not thy chariot, nor the smoking axle of the car that Phaethon would drive. If thou wilt use thy fires right wisely, Apollo, come hither, and lay thy glories in my breast!" Thus amorously breathes the wanton Earth. . . .

Let us now examine some of the materials out of which Milton has put together this passage.

The pervasive influence, far and away, is that of Ovid, who in diverse places had much to say on the subject of the Sun-god, Phoebus. Thus, one of the best-known tales in the *Metamorphoses* deals with the fatal request of Phaethon, the son of Phoebus, for permission from his father to drive for one day the unruly horses of the Sun from east to west. Phoebus reluctantly consents but, before he does so, he warns his son of the ardors of the journey, particularly of the fearsome western decline.

tunc etiam quae me subiectis excipit undis,
ne ferar in praeceps, Tethys solet ipsa vereri [24]

Met. 2.68–69

Then even Tethys, who receives me in her underlying waters, is wont to fear lest I fall headlong.

Here, then, we have the genesis of the first two and a half lines of the passage from Milton: *subiectis excipit undis* becomes *Hesperiis recipit . . . aquis*, perhaps under the additional influence of a line from the Fourth Book of the *Metamorphoses* (line 214), where the Sun is again associated with the epithet "Hesperian":

---

[23] The translation, here and elsewhere, of Milton's Latin poems is taken from the new Cambridge edition (1941), edited by Harris F. Fletcher. Fletcher adopts, with modifications, the translation of W. V. Moody as revised by E. K. Rand. For the text of the Latin poems and the text of *Paradise Lost* I have used the University of Illinois edition of *John Milton's Complete Poetical Works* (4 vols.), a photographic facsimile, edited by Harris F. Fletcher (Urbana, 1943–48). The Latin poems appear in the first volume (1943); *Paradise Lost* appears in the third (1948).

[24] Quotations from the *Metamorphoses* are from the text and translation of Frank J. Miller in the Loeb edition, 1936 (first printing, 1916).

> Axe sub Hesperio sunt pascua Solis equorum:

Beneath the western skies lie the pastures of the Sun's horses.

or, more likely still, of a verse from Ovid's *Fasti* (2.73):

> Proximus Hesperias Titan abiturus in undas

When the next sun, before he sinks into the western waves. . . .[25]

Milton has simply taken the words out of Phoebus' mouth and given them to Tellus, who, in his version, is addressing Phoebus.

In the terminology of Renaissance schoolmasters, this kind of adaptation was known as "varying." Another example occurs in the same line (82). Ovid has the phrase *Caerula mater* (*Met.* 13.288), and so does Horace (*Epodes* 13.16), but in both instances the phrase is applied to Thetis, the goddess of the sea who was the mother of Achilles. Milton simply transfers the phrase to Tethys, another goddess of the sea. The transference of epithets and descriptive phrases from one application to another was part of the mechanics of imitation. Milton's *Caerula mater*, we may note in passing, is not merely ornamental; it establishes another fertility symbol in Tethys, the Sea-mother, as opposed to Tellus, the Earth-mother, both rival claimants for the affections of the Sun-god. Tellus is basing her appeal to Phoebus on the received notion that fire and water are inimical to one another, and this is her way of reminding Phoebus that no union of his with Tethys could ever be a fruitful one. *Caerula mater* has been effectively absorbed into its new context. No one would contend that it is a particularly subtle borrowing, but the passage would perhaps lose something without it.

The third line imitates, in the Ovidian manner and even in his very word order, a favorite rhetorical trick, exemplified by this verse from the *Heroides* (6.47):

> Quid mihi cum Minyis, quid cum Dodonide pinu?

What had I with the Minyae, or Dodona's pine? [26]

But why Milton's *Tartesside lymphâ*? In classical Latin poetry there are few occurrences of the epithet *Tartessius*. Ovid, however, has it in the Fourteenth Book of the *Metamorphoses* (line 416):

> Sparserat occiduus Tartessia litora Phoebus,

Now the setting sun had bathed the Tartessian shores. . . .

The presence of *Phoebus* in the verse leaves little doubt that this is the source of Milton's borrowing. It is surprising that Milton should be able to recall this association of Phoebus with *Tartessia litora*,

---

[25] Sir James G. Frazer's translation in the Loeb edition, 1931.
[26] Grant Showerman's translation in the Loeb edition, 1921.

since here Phoebus has almost entirely lost his mythological character, becoming a mere poetical variant for the word "sun," a mere synonym, *occiduus . . . Phoebus.* But Milton remembered, and the phrase, slightly varied to fit the new context (*litora* plainly would not do), reappears in his poem. The borrowing is a testimonial to his memory and to the freedom with which his mind ranged about in the *Metamorphoses.*

But Milton is not yet done with that poem. Near the end of the passage, Tellus invites a comparison between what her own fate might be, if Phoebus should descend to court her, and the fates of Semele and Phaethon.

> Nec me (crede mihi) terrent Semelëia fata,
> Nec Phäetonteo fumidus axis equo;
>
> *El.* 5.91–92

Believe me, I fear not Semele's fate; I fear not thy chariot, nor the smoking axle of the car that Phaethon would drive.

What one remarks about these two allusions to Semele and Phaethon is not their appropriateness, for one would expect that, but their compression. It is a commonplace of Milton criticism that, as he grew artistically more mature, his mythological allusions exhibit more and more a tendency toward compression. That is true, although one must remember that, if Milton were to observe a due decorum, the treatment of mythology in an Ovidian imitation like the *Fifth Elegy* would necessarily be different from that in an epic, or even in poems like *Comus* or *Lycidas.* Perhaps it has been the heavy and pervasive mythological element in the elegies which has obscured the fact that Milton, even in the Latin poems written while he was still an undergraduate at Cambridge, was capable of an impressive economy in his employment of myth. *Semelëia fata* is the precursor of such highly condensed expressions in *Paradist Lost* as "Atlantean shoulders," "Typhoean rage," and "Circean call." The technical advance demonstrable in the phrases from *Paradise Lost* does not lie in their verbal compression but in the fact that they generate more meaning within their context; they are interpretative as well as descriptive (see below, pp. 95–96).

The striking phrase *Phäetonteo fumidus axis equo* is interesting for another reason. It is an adaptation of Ovid's

> nil illo fertur volucrum moderator equorum
> post Phaethonteos vidisse dolentius ignes.
>
> *Met.* 4.245–46

Naught more pitiful than that sight, they say, did the driver of the swift steeds see since Phaëthon's burning death.

Milton's phrase varying Ovid's *Phaethonteos . . . ignes*. Here the
borrowing would not have been so easy to detect had it not been that
the epithet *Phaethonteos* is almost unique in classical literature and
that no poet except Ovid had associated it directly with the idea of
burning. By means of the verbal echo Milton is able to work still
another mythological thread into his pattern of allusion. The two
lines from Ovid come near the end of a story which relates how the
jealousy of Clytie resulted in the death of Leucothoe, slain by her
irate father. Both were rivals for the love of Phoebus and both were
goddesses of the sea. The newly introduced myth has an obvious
relevance to the substance of the lines from the *Fifth Elegy*, and the
purpose of the verbal echo stands revealed.

In the concluding lines of Tellus' plea,

> Cum tu Phoebe tuo sapientius uteris igni,
> Huc ades & gremio lumina pone meo.
>
> *El.* 5.93–94

If thou wilt use thy fires right wisely, Apollo, come hither, and lay thy glories
in my breast!

there is a return to the Phaethon story itself. The allusion is to the
Earth's agonized protest to Jove against the use to which Phaethon
is putting the fires of the Sun (see *Met.* 2.272–300). We may note the
ambiguity present in the word *igni* — "fire" in its ordinary meaning
and "fire" in a colloquial sexual sense — which helps to color the
interpretation we are to put on the word *lumina* in the next line; the
rays of the sun are a source of life as well as of light. The word is
placed in a context which unmistakably brings out a meaning already
latent in it from its use by classical authors. It is in keeping with
the general tone of the passage, and indeed of the whole poem, that
Milton should stress the fertilizing, and not the illuminating, proper-
ties of the sun.

Generally speaking, when Milton employs the device of the verbal
echo in the earlier Latin poems, his aim is to work upon the emotions
of his readers, seldom upon their intellect. "Emotion," says W. B.
Yeats in words which virtually describe what Milton is doing with
mythology in the Latin poems, "grows intoxicating and delightful
after it has been enriched with the memory of old emotions, with
all the uncounted flavours of old experience. . . ." [27] To call these
old emotions once again into the service of poetry is the characteristic purpose of the classical allusions in the elegies. Let us take, for
a final example, the fifth line of our passage (line 85):

---

[27] *Discoveries* (Dundrum, 1907), pp. 28–29.

Frigora Phoebe meâ melius captabis in umbrâ,

A better coolness, Apollo, thou mayst find in my shade.

which echoes a phrase in Virgil's *First Eclogue* (line 53):

et fontes sacros frigus captabis opacum.[28]

[Amid] holy springs thou wilt woo the coolness of the shade.

The effect of this echo is to make almost irresistibly attractive the
sensuality of Tellus by associating it with the serene, lovely, and idyllic world of Virgil's shepherds, Meliboeus and Tityrus. The echo
draws back, as it were, the curtain which opens out on that world
where "amid familiar streams and holy springs thou wilt woo the
coolness of the shade: here the hedge that ever keeps thy neighbour's
boundary, where bees of Hybla feed their fill on the willow-blossom,
shall often with light murmuring lull thee into sleep: here under the
lofty rock shall rise the leaf-gatherer's song: nor all the while shall
the hoarse wood-pigeons, thy delight, or the turtle on the elm's aëry
top cease to moan" (lines 52–59). The idea of a lulling to sleep, we
may observe, is present in both passages, reinforcing the notion that
Milton had the context of the Virgilian phrase in mind and wished
to have it in the minds of his readers as well.

The late Professor E. K. Rand, in his brilliant essay entitled "Milton in Rustication," pays ardent tribute to Milton's genius as an
imitator. Of the *Fifth Elegy*, he writes:

It is Pagan from beginning to end, joyous in spirit, sensuous in flavor, perfect in form. Really if Milton had written it on musty parchment and had
somebody discover it, the Classical pundits of his day would have proved
beyond question by all the tests of scholarship that a lost work of Ovid
had come to light. So with most of the other pieces that he collected in a
tiny book of "elegies." To write them he must have known his Ovid virtually by heart, not merely the *Metamorphoses*, which then and now make the
best possible introduction to the world of romance and human charm preserved in the old Greek myths, but all the poems of Ovid, *Fasti* and *Ibis*,
as well as the poor verses of lamentation poured forth on the shores of the
Black Sea, and of course, as Milton is writing elegy, the love poems, *Amores*
with *Heroides*, and the Art of Love.[29]

This is high praise and from a most authoritative source. But Professor Rand's comment, while it proclaims the distinctive merits of the
Fifth Elegy, also exposes its limitations. The poem is all Ovid; there
is little in it of Milton at all. So close an imitation of another writer's
style can only arise from a profound understanding of the principles

---

[28] The text of the *Ecloques* I have used is that of T. L. Papillon and A. E. Haigh
(New York, n.d.); the translation is John W. Mackail's in the Modern Library
edition of *Virgil's Works: The Aeneid, Eclogues, Georgics* (New York, n.d.).

[29] *SP*, XIX (1922), 111.

upon which that style has been formed, and such an understanding augurs well for the future. But, for all that, the *Fifth Elegy* remains a splendid tour de force. Once, however, in the poem and, as far as I have been able to determine, once only, Milton shows a flash of that creative insight which makes for the highest order of imitation.

Of the one hundred and forty lines of the poem, the first twenty-four constitute a kind of proem, in which the poet announces that spring has arrived and that, with its coming, he has felt the first mysterious stirrings of the impulse to return to the composition of poetry. The rest of the poem satisfies that impulse in the praise of spring which, as we have seen, Milton pictures as a time of universal love-making, fertility, and rebirth, and commemorates in a diction and imagery rhapsodically and pervasively sexual, as befits his theme. The first twenty-four lines, therefore, posed something of a problem. How was he to link up these lines, so pure and exalted in their fervent Platonism, with the rest of the poem in such a way as to achieve an essential unity of impression? He decided on a bold measure, one which perhaps he would not have attempted had he not been twenty years old and writing an Ovidian imitation in the first quarter of the seventeenth century. Spring has arrived and, writes Milton,

> Fallor? an & nobis redeunt in carmina vires,
> Ingeniumque mihi munere veris adest?
> Munere veris adest, iterumque vigescit ab illo
> (Quis putet) atque aliquod iam sibi poscit opus.
>   *El.* 5.5–8

Do I mistake? Doth not also my strength in song return? At the spring's gift is not inspiration here? At the spring's gift 'tis here! Again it gathers strength therefrom (who could believe it?) and looks about for some nobler task.

These lines seem innocent and decorous enough. But, in point of fact, Milton's *poscit opus* is a carefully designed reminiscence of the phrase as it appears in the Third Book of Ovid's *Amores* (3.7.68) in a brutally frank passage describing the return of the poet's potency after an initial sexual experience with his mistress. In the light of the Ovidian context from which Milton has borrowed, the four lines that have just been quoted from the *Fifth Elegy* are invested with a new and startling set of implications which not only play an important part in the poem's total meaning but which also help to establish a unity of tone, theme, and metaphor. This is imitation in the true sense — creative imitation, as some modern critics have called it — and it embraces critical principles which were as generally accepted in Milton's own day as they are at the present time.

It is well to remind ourselves of this fact, for "imitation" is a word which will inevitably have unpleasant or at least misleading connotations for most modern readers. It seems to imply that, by diligent searching, formulae may be found for constructing a synthetic poem. The Renaissance grammar-school methods of studying and imitating the classical authors may even appear to have been based upon that premise. And it is no doubt true that the system did tend to encourage the servile and indiscriminate imitation of those authors. One could not reasonably expect much more from the average boy of grammar-school age. But if in practice, in school and out of school, there was much of that slavish borrowing we today would regard as plagiarism, nothing is more evident than that Renaissance critics and educators were fiercely and unalterably opposed to it, as defeating the ends of true imitation. They accepted without cavil Quintilian's dictum: "imitation alone is not sufficient" (*imitatio per se ipsa non sufficit*).[30]

Underlying and sustaining the Renaissance theory of imitation was the belief that a literary inheritance constituted a common property, *publica materies*, in the well-known phrase of Horace. The work of a poet belonged to the reading and writing public just as soon as he issued it to the world. Hence, his contemporaries or successors were entitled to borrow what they pleased, provided that their motive was not simple theft. But the mere borrowing of verbal, stylistic, and structural details from other poets did not in itself constitute true imitation. Indeed, writes Quintilian, whose *Institutes* were the prime source from which the Renaissance derived its doctrine of imitation, it is a "positive disgrace" (*Turpe etiam illud est*) for a poet to stake all his claim to poetic distinction on this sort of imitation (10.2.7). Furthermore, such a poet can anticipate at best only a limited success. "For the man whose aim is to prove himself better than another, even if he does not surpass him, may hope to equal him. But he can never hope to equal him, if he thinks it his duty merely to tread in his footsteps: for the mere follower must always lag behind" (10.2.10). The copy will be to the original as the shadow to the substance (*ut umbra corpore*). On the other hand, by entering into a conscious rivalry with some great writer of the past, the imitator will inevitably be inspired to his finest achievement. Had not Plato "striven with heart and soul to contest the prize" with Homer, says Longinus, he might never have realized his potential greatness.[31] Above all, the imitator must endeavor to recapture "the force of style

---

[30] *Institutio Oratoria*, ed. and transl. H. E. Butler (Loeb edition, 1921–22), 10.2.4. All citations from Quintilian in this study are to Butler's edition.
[31] *On the Sublime*, 13.4.

and invention" (*vim dicendi atque inventionis*) inherent in the original.[32]

The purpose of the imitator should, therefore, be to secure fresh and original effects through a revitalization of the borrowed materials and, to succeed in this purpose, he must try to see by "what art, by what method, such and such was achieved by the author, in order that he himself with a similar artifice may accomplish his own intention in his own work," to quote the Renaissance scholar and critic, Juan Luis Vives.[33] The example par excellence of Renaissance critics for original imitation was Virgil. According to Donatus, whose commentary on Virgil would have been familiar to most schoolboys, either through their own reading or the exposition of their masters, Quintus Octavius Avitus had compiled eight volumes of Virgilian parallels and Perellius Laertes an anthology of his so-called "thefts." Yet no responsible critics had ever accused Virgil of plagiarism. He had simply demonstrated better than anyone else that, in the words of Macrobius (who himself lists hundreds of Virgil's borrowings), "the fruit of reading is to emulate what one finds good in others, and by suitable adaptation to convert what one most admires in others to one's own uses." [34]

Centuries later, an English critic, the sage and serious Roger Ascham, was to find the method of Macrobius something less than satisfactory, and what he has to say on the subject is quite illuminating. After calling attention to the wish of Erasmus that some ambitious scholar would do for Cicero and Demosthenes what Macrobius had done for Virgil and Homer, Ascham wryly adds: "even so, onlie to point out and nakedlie to joyne togither their sentences, with no farder declaring the maner and way, how the one doth folow the other, were but a colde helpe, to the encrease of learning." [35] In a later passage, he returns to the attack: "But all these, with *Macrobius, Hessus*, and other, be no more than common porters, carriers, and bringers of matter and stuffe together. They order nothing: They lay before you what is done: they do not teach you, how it is done. They busie not them selves with forme of buildyng. . . . " [36] Readers like Roger Ascham would not only agree with T. S. Eliot's dictum

[32] *Inst. Orat.* 10.2.16.

[33] Foster Watson, *Vives: On Education* (Cambridge, Eng., 1913), p. 195. The quotation is from Watson's translation of Vives' *De Tradendis Disciplinis*, a treatise published at Antwerp in 1531.

[34] *Saturnalia*, 6.1. Quoted by Harold O. White, *Plagiarism and Imitation During the English Renaissance* (Cambridge, Mass., 1935), p. 5.

[35] *The Scholemaster*, ed. John E. B. Mayor (London, 1863), p. 145.

[36] Ascham, p. 154.

that the most individual parts of an artist's work are often those "in which the dead poets, his ancestors, assert their immortality most vigorously," [37] they would be eager to resolve the paradox, to discover, if they could, why it should be so and not otherwise.

The poet, of course, travels the road of imitation at his own risk, and risks there are on each side, at every turn. It was Virgil who is supposed to have said: "It is easier to steal the club from Hercules than to take a line from Homer." In other words, by borrowing from the work of his precedessors, the imitative poet is inviting the sort of comparison by which his poem must stand or fall. The borrowed materials, instead of improving the poem, may actually demean it by focusing attention upon its general inferiority. The point is well illustrated by an experience which Montaigne relates. Of a book he had been reading, he says:

I had been languidly crawling after French words, so fleshless, so bloodless, so void of matter and sense, that they were truly only French words; at the end of a long and tedious journey I came across a passage that was rich, sublime, and elevated to the very clouds. If I had found the declivity easy and the ascent a little gradual, it would have been excusable: it was a precipice so perpendicular and abrupt that, at the first six words, I knew that I was flying into another world. From thence I described the quagmire from which I had come, so low and deep, that I never since had the heart to descend to it again. Were I to stuff one of my essays with those rich spoils, it would throw too strong a light on the stupidity of the others.[38]

The inferior poet who risks specific comparisons with his betters is foolhardy indeed.

From first to last Milton was, in the true Renaissance sense, an imitative poet. As everyone knows, he was little more than a boy when he set it down that the ambition of his life was to become an epic poet.[39] From this goal he never wavered in a long and arduous apprenticeship to the Muse. During his school days and at the University, it was Ovid who was his master, and those other "smooth Elegiack Poets, whereof the Schooles are not scarce. Whom both for the pleasing sound of their numerous writing, which in imitation I found most easie, and most agreeable to natures part in me, and for their matter which what it is, there be few who know not, I was so allur'd to read, that no recreation came to me better welcome." [40]

---

[37] "Tradition and the Individual Talent" in *Selected Essays* (New York, 1932), p. 4.

[38] "Of the Education of Children" in *The Essays of Montaigne*, transl. E. J. Trechmann (London, 1935), I, 144.

[39] See lines 29–52 of the *Vacation Exercise*, written in 1628.

[40] "Apology for Smectymnuus" in *Works*, III, pt. I, p. 302.

Later on, it was Spenser and Virgil and, as Professor Rand has shown, at first the growing and not the grown Virgil, the Virgil of the *Eclogues* and the *Georgics*.[41] From Milton's own statements or from the inferences which may be drawn from them, but, most of all, from the evidence of his poetry, it may be confidently asserted that there has never been a poet more supremely conscious of a high poetic destiny or more deliberate, painstaking, and assiduous in his preparations to realize it. This was not pride but genuine humility.

Like all his contemporaries, Milton believed that poems are of different kinds and that each kind is governed by its own laws. The nature of the poet's intention determined the kind and the choice of kind determined the models he set before him. Furthermore, just as there was operative in the world of man and of nature a well-defined hierarchy of "degree," so a similar hierarchy existed in the realm of poetry. This belief that poems differ in kind and value, one should add, did not stem from a sterile authoritarianism. It grew out of the intelligent study of the great classical writers. The early masterpieces were regarded as having set a pattern for each literary kind, the excellence of which could be demonstrated by reason and experience, as well as by the practice of the Roman authors themselves, who had constantly imitated the acknowledged masters in their respective genres. The principle is aesthetically sound. The poet who strayed too far from the pattern was not only defying experience, he was also in a sense betraying the reader by depriving him of the pleasures of recognition, contrast, and comparison. Of course, the poet should not go to the other extreme and adhere slavishly to his model. "Imitation," says Pope, "does not hinder invention: we may observe the rules of nature, and write in the spirit of those who have best hit upon them; without taking the same track, beginning in the same manner, and following the main of their story almost step by step."[42] It is for following the latter course in his *Prince Arthur* that John Dennis takes Blackmore to task.[43]

At the top of the hierarchy, almost all critics agreed, stood the epic. Many readers today will find it far from easy to appreciate the importance which Milton's contemporaries ascribed to the function of the epic poet. But when Dryden wrote that "A heroic poem, truly such, is undoubtedly the greatest work which the soul of man is ca-

---

[41] Rand, pp. 123 ff.

[42] *The "Iliad" of Homer*, transl. Alexander Pope. A new edition, by Gilbert Wakefield (London, 1796), Vol. I. See the section entitled "Notes Preliminary."

[43] *The Critical Works of John Dennis*, ed. Edward N. Hooker (Baltimore, Md., 1939), I, 60.

pable to perform," he was speaking not only for himself but for his century.[44] It was of the epic, too, that Milton was thinking when he wrote that the poet, to succeed, must himself be a "true Poem";[45] his function is like that of the priest and his character should be as spotless.[46] Above all, he must be prodigiously learned. The man who held such a sublime conception of the epic, who hoped some day to do for his own native language "what the greatest and choycest wits of *Athens*, *Rome*, or modern *Italy*, and the Hebrews of old" had done for theirs,[47] was not likely to enter upon so grave a responsibility lightly. And we know that he did not.

As for the noblest practitioners of the epic, there was no disagreement whatsoever. "Only the Bible," writes Basil Willey, "could claim a greater share of reverence than Homer and Virgil." [48] It was perhaps this very reverence for Homer and Virgil, together with the popularity of romantic epics like the *Faerie Queene* or the *Orlando Furioso*, which brought about a cleavage between theory and practice. For although all critics were agreed that Homer and Virgil were the most suitable models, only a few attempts were made to write epics clearly and unmistakably in the tradition of those poets, and all but one or two resulted in failures. Perhaps poets were intimidated by the imputed greatness of Homer and Virgil and did not wish to be measured by their standards. This would seem to be a logical inference. Only a very great poet, like Milton, or a very presumptuous one, like Blackmore or Cowley, would dare to expose himself to the inevitable comparisons.

Of the two, it was generally conceded in Milton's day that Virgil made a more suitable model than Homer. First, as everyone knows, the Homeric poems were designed to be recited, and this fact had necessarily conditioned their style and structure. Both the *Iliad* and the *Odyssey* are made up of episodes relatively complete in themselves, episodes which could, when the need arose, be detached from the poems and recited individually. Their oral patterning is likewise mirrored in the constant epithets and stock phrases, the repetition of lines and whole passages, the stylized diction, the stereotyped descriptions, even the occasional carelessness in matters of detail. Con-

---

[44] *Essays of John Dryden*, ed. W. P. Ker (Oxford, 1900), II, 154. And see Ker's Introduction, I, xv–xix, on the reputation of the epic during the seventeenth century.

[45] "Apology for Smectymnuus" in *Works*, III, pt. I, p. 303.

[46] See the *Sixth Elegy*, written in 1629, especially lines 77–78.

[47] "The Reason of Church-Government" in *Works*, III, pt. I, p. 236.

[48] *The Seventeenth Century Background* (New York, 1949; first edition, 1934), p. 219.

sequently, although Homer was believed to excel in his vivid narrative and in the intensity and variety of his emotional effects, Virgil was regarded as the more finished craftsman; the *Aeneid*, men thought, possessed fewer artistic blemishes and moreover a structure which lent itself more readily to effective imitation. Second, the *Aeneid* had been studied much more closely. As we have seen, it had the most important place in the grammar-school curriculum. If Milton could safely presuppose a close, working knowledge of any one poet, that poet was Virgil. But he could not make a similar assumption in the case of Homer. He could assume a certain familiarity with the main outlines of the Homeric story and some knowledge of episodic detail, possibly derived from translations, but in the average reader no such exact verbal knowledge as he could assume in the case of Virgil. This is important, because the full effectiveness of any borrowing can scarcely be realized unless the reader is able to recognize an allusion or an echo when it occurs — the necessary first step in the evaluative process. Third, whereas Homer had no known literary antecedents, Virgil had many and most of them were known to the poets and scholars of the Renaissance. It was, therefore, possible to study Virgil at work and, as we have seen, Virgil's use of his literary forebears had always been a source of great interest. And, finally, there was the powerful influence wielded over Renaissance criticism by Vida and Scaliger, both of whom regarded Virgil as without a peer among poets, ancient or modern.

There was hence every reason why Milton should choose Homer and Virgil, particularly the latter, as his models. What made his choice of those poets virtually mandatory, however, was not so much the critical tradition or his lifelong ambition to emulate them as it was his sure realization that, for the fullest expression of his genius and his theme, he could not do without Homer and Virgil. Only against the background of their work could the whole significance of his own contribution to epic development be grasped. The meaning of *Paradise Lost* is inextricably bound up with the meanings of the *Aeneid* and the Homeric poems, and cannot be entirely understood unless they are taken into account.

CHAPTER TWO

Not Less but More Heroic

At the heart of every true epic is the attempt to express a way of life, and an attitude toward it, which will enable man to live out his days "upon the rack of this tough world," if not exactly happily, at least with honor and dignity. Let us look for a moment at the *Iliad*. In it Homer depicts a primitive age when the conditions for survival fostered an attachment to self which transcended all other loyalties. Primitive self-attachment chiefly displays itself in the pursuit of personal honor and glory. The warriors of the *Iliad* fight and die, or live and suffer, not absolutely out of any allegiance to prince or cause or country — not even out of a sense of what is right and just — but to win lasting fame for themselves. Their philosophy is implicit in the well-known words which the Trojan Sarpedon addresses to his friend Glaukos before they hurl themselves on the Greek defenses:

> Glaukos, wherefore have we twain the chiefest honour, — seats of honour, and messes, and full cups in Lykia, and all men look on us as gods? And wherefore hold we a great demesne by the banks of Xanthos, a fair demesne of orchard-land, and wheat-bearing tilth? Therefore now it behoveth us to take our stand in the first rank of the Lykians, and encounter fiery battle, that certain of the well-corseleted Lykians may say, "Verily our kings that rule Lykia be no inglorious men, they that eat fat sheep, and drink the choice wine honey-sweet: nay, but they are also of excellent might, for they war in the foremost ranks of the Lykians." Ah, friend, if once escaped from this battle we were for ever to be ageless and immortal, neither would I fight myself in the foremost ranks, nor would I send thee into the war that giveth men renown, but now — for assuredly ten thousands fates of death do every way beset us, and these no mortal may escape nor avoid — now let us go forward, whether we shall give glory to other men, or others to us.[1]

In the world of Homer there were only two ways for an individual to achieve lasting glory: by displaying valor in action or by dying a heroic death — in either, to be "ever the boldest . . . and pre-eminent among others" (*Iliad*, p. 208). This was the cornerstone of the

---

[1] *The Complete Works of Homer, the Iliad and the Odyssey.* The *Iliad* done into English prose by Andrew Lang, Walter Leaf, and Ernest Myers. The *Odyssey* done into English prose by S. H. Butcher and Andrew Lang. Modern Library (New York, n.d.), pp. 219–20. All translations of Homer are taken from this text, hereafter cited as *Iliad* or *Odyssey*.

heroic creed, and the true measure of a man's achievement in the only world he would probably ever know.

Here, too, is the reason why the action of the *Iliad* largely resolves itself into patterns of individual exploits and clashes, by no means limited to the field of battle. In portraying his action in this way, Homer was faithfully mirroring the spirit of glory-seeking individualism which characterized the heroic age. Hence, the stories of Homer, and the characters who participate in them, do not explicitly stand for anything outside themselves; they are self-contained and self-sufficient. In the *Iliad*, for example, larger issues, where they exist, tend to be lost or at least obscured in the swirl of individual activity and, in the end, appropriately enough, we are left to infer the Fall of Troy from the death of Hector. It is not the Fall of Troy but the wrath of Achilles and its consequences which is the subject of the *Iliad* and its unifying principle. This is clearly set forth in the exordium of the poem, and is subsequently justified by its structure.[2]

Sing, goddess, the wrath of Achilles Peleus' son, the ruinous wrath that brought on the Achaians woes innumerable, and hurled down into Hades many strong souls of heroes, and gave their bodies to be a prey to dogs and all winged fowls; and so the counsel of Zeus wrought out its accomplishment from the day when first strife parted Atreides king of men and noble Achilles.

Who then among the gods set the twain at strife and variance? Even the son of Leto and Zeus . . . [*Iliad*, p. 1].

In the *Odyssey* there is even less justification for the imaginative reconstruction of its events in terms of conscious meaning. Imposing a figure as Odysseus is, exciting as are his adventures, and as brilliantly told as they are, in the last analysis he "bears with him only his fortunes and those of the companions of his adventure; he ends his career as he begins it, the chief of a small island, which derives all its importance solely from its early association with his fortunes."[3] This is not to say, of course, that the *Odyssey* and the *Iliad* are lacking in symbolic values. But these values are not overtly present in the poems themselves; they reside somewhere outside the poems, in the correspondence of things in universal nature, and in the human mind which perceives that correspondence.

Like Homer, Virgil wished to write an epic which would stimulate the patriotism of his countrymen by awakening an interest in the glories of the national past. His motive for writing in the Homeric

---

[2] For an analysis of this structure, see especially C. M. Bowra's *Tradition and Design in the Iliad* (Oxford, 1930), pp. 16 ff.

[3] William Y. Sellar, *Roman Poets of the Augustan Age* (Oxford, 1897), p. 213.

tradition must have been partly personal, partly aesthetic. In view of the final achievement, no one can doubt that he recognized from the beginning the potential usefulness of the tradition. But it would have been strange, too, if a poet of his genius had not also been animated by a purely personal ambition to be acclaimed a second Homer, the highest honor to which a Roman poet could aspire. Virgil must have seen clearly enough, however, that he could never hope to attain to that splendid eminence by writing in the Homeric manner and from the Homeric point of view. The time for that was long past. Hundreds of years had gone by and, in the meantime, the conception of man and his place in the social and universal order had undergone a drastic revision. The problem for Virgil was how to make the Homeric tradition valid for his own time and country. In the magnificent exordium of the *Aeneid*, Virgil clearly indicates his indebtedness to the tradition and suggests the ways he is going to depart from it. This exordium is in a very real sense the seed pod of the whole poem, and it will therefore repay a close study. Here are the lines with which the *Aeneid* opens:

> Arma virumque cano, Troiae qui primus ab oris
> Italiam fato profugus Lavinaque venit
> litora, multum ille et terris iactatus et alto
> vi superum, saevae memorem Iunonis ob iram,
> multa quoque et bello passus, dum conderet urbem
> inferretque deos Latio, genus unde Latinum
> Albanique patres atque altae moenia Romae.[4]
>
> 1.1–7

I sing of arms and the man who came of old, a fated wanderer, from the coasts of Troy to Italy and the shore of Lavinium; hard driven on land and on the deep by the violence of heaven, by reason of cruel Juno's unforgetful anger, and hard bestead in war also, ere he might found a city and carry his gods into Latium; from whom is the Latin race, the Lords of Alba, and high-embattled Rome.

On the surface this passage would appear to be nothing more than a conventional statement of the subject matter of the poem. But for educated Romans, who knew Homer as English schoolboys were later to know Virgil, these verses would have had many more important meanings. In them Virgil skillfully compresses the substance of both Homeric invocations. Indeed, the opening phrase *Arma virumque cano* is a brilliant distillation of the distinguishing marks of the

---

[4] Latin citations from Virgil's *Aeneid* are to John W. Mackail's edition, with an introduction and commentary (Oxford, 1930). The translation, here and elsewhere, is also his, as it is given in the Modern Library edition of his *Virgil's Works*.

Homeric epic, *arma* suggesting the idea of heroic action on the field of battle and *vir* reminding us of the importance which Homer's world ascribed to individual prowess. More than that, however, *arma* suggests Achilles, and *vir*, Odysseus. Can we doubt that the Latin word *vir* deliberately echoes the Greek word *anthropos*, as Homer had used it in the opening verses of the *Odyssey*?

Tell me, Muse, of that man [*anthropos*], so ready at need, who wandered far and wide, after he had sacked the sacred citadel of Troy, and many were the men whose towns he saw and whose mind he learnt, yea, and many the woes he suffered in his heart upon the deep, striving to win his own life and the return of his company [*Odyssey*, p. 1].

In both the Greek and Latin a strong positional emphasis is allowed to fall on the word and, more significantly, in both cases the name of the hero is momentarily withheld.[5] Virgil is pitting the worth of his own hero against that of both Achilles and Odysseus.

Other striking correspondences confirm the impression that Virgil had studied the Homeric invocations closely and had them in his mind, if not actually before him, when he composed the exordium to the *Aeneid*. Like the *Odyssey*, Virgil's poem is to recite the adventures and suffering of a hero whose sea wanderings begin from fallen Troy, and who will be "hard bestead in war also," like the heroes of the *Iliad*. But the Homeric echoes are present for a more subtle purpose than that, as certain key words and phrases make plain. Aeneas is no ordinary wanderer; he is a "fated wanderer" (*fato profugus*), destined in the end, after much toil, to be the founder of a race and city which will one day establish a new world order.

. . . genus unde Latinum
Albanique patres atque altae moenia Romae.

1.6–7

From whom is the Latin race, the lords of Alba, and high-embattled Rome.

By echoing, in his use of the word *profugus*, the invocation of the *Odyssey* (Odysseus, too, is described as a wanderer), Virgil is reminding his readers that the motive which impels Odysseus to seek his homeland is uncomplicated by other considerations than his longing for wife and children and his own safety and that of his followers. In other words, Virgil is making a subdued and respectful plea for the superior greatness of his subject as well as suggesting the ways in which he wants it interpreted. Perhaps to sharpen the contrast between the motives of Odysseus and Aeneas, Virgil makes the entry of the latter into Italy, in a sense, also a "home-coming." We learn be-

---

[5] See below, pp. 35–36.

fore the poem has fairly got under way that Aeneas' countryman, Antenor, had established a settlement in Italy some years before his arrival (1.242–49).

Having set forth his subject, Virgil proceeds to invoke the Muse.

> Musa, mihi causas memora, quo numine laeso
> quidve dolens regina deum tot volvere casus
> insignem pietate virum, tot adire labores
> impulerit. tantaene animis caelestibus irae?
>
> 1.8–11

Muse, tell me why, for what attaint of her deity, or in what vexation, did the Queen of heaven urge on a man excellent in goodness to circle through all those afflictions, to face all those toils? Is anger so fierce in celestial spirits?

The rhetorical question with which Virgil concludes his invocation, as his editors have noted, is an imitation of Homer, specifically these lines which follow hard upon the Homeric invocation.

Who then among the gods set the twain at strife and variance? Even the son of Leto and of Zeus; for he in anger at the king sent a sore plague upon the host, that the folk began to perish, because Atreides had done dishonour to Chryses the priest [*Iliad*, p. 1].

But again Virgil is not using a convention idly. As before, he is using it to imply a contrast, this time with the *Iliad*. The motive which led Apollo, the son of Leto and Zeus, to incite the quarrel between Agamemnon and Achilles was essentially a personal one. He wished to avenge the wrong done to his priest Chryses. Juno's hatred of Aeneas and his followers, though it had a personal aspect, was in the main political, as Virgil is at great pains to make clear. Carthage is dear to Juno and she had placed it under her protection. It is the land she favors above all others.

> Urbs antiqua fuit, Tyrii tenuere coloni,
> Karthago, Italiam contra Tiberinaque longe
> ostia, dives opum studiisque asperrima belli;
> quam Iuno fertur terris magis omnibus unam
> posthabita coluisse Samo: hic illius arma,
> hic currus fuit; hoc regnum dea gentibus esse,
> si qua fata sinant, iam tum tenditque fovetque.
> progeniem sed enim Troiano a sanguine duci
> audierat Tyrias olim quae verteret arces;
> hinc populum late regem belloque superbum
> venturum excidio Libyae: sic volvere Parcas.
>
> 1.12–22

There was a city of ancient days that Tyrian settlers dwelt in, Carthage, over against Italy and the Tiber mouths afar; plenteous of wealth, and most grim in the arts of war; wherein, they say, alone beyond all other lands had Juno her seat, and held Samos itself less dear. Here was her armour, here her chariot; even now, if fate permit, the goddess strives to nurture it for dominion over the nations. Nevertheless she had heard that a race was issuing of the blood of Troy, which sometime should overthrow her Tyrian fortress; from it should come a people, lord of lands and tyrannous in war, the destroyer of Libya: thus the Fates unrolled their volume.

The introduction of the political motif thus becomes the occasion for a swift glimpse far into the future to a time when the descendants of Aeneas shall accomplish a work of destruction fated from the beginning, *sic volvere Parcas.* Mr. C. S. Lewis has called attention to the way the key words in this passage operate to spread the story in time and place, and to link it up with the notion of destiny — *antiqua, longe, regnum, fata, olim, late, Parcas.*[6] Then, in the next eleven lines (23–33), Virgil takes us into the past, to the Fall of Troy and to the mythical origins of Juno's hatred for the Trojans. By encompassing, in twenty-two lines, such a vast sweep of time and space, he is deliberately investing his poem with a proper magnitude, a magnitude which will enable him to emphasize more strongly both the difficulties that had to be overcome before Rome could be founded and also the role which a providential destiny had played in shaping her future greatness. Appropriately, this tremendous surge, forward and backward in time, ends with the weighty verse, *tantae molis erat Romanam condere gentem* (1.33; "Such work was it to found the Roman people").

This linking of the past with the present, this endowment of legendary and historical events with contemporary significance, all achieved within the framework of the Homeric epic, was Virgil's great contribution to epic development. Throughout the *Aeneid*, the reader is constantly aware that neither the characters nor the actions in which they are revealed have their complete meaning in themselves. Thus Aeneas is not simply Aeneas; he is the prototypal Roman, a true symbol of Roman *virtus* and greatness, *attollens humero famamque et fata nepotum* (8.731; "lifting on his shoulders the destined glories of his children"). When he leaves Dido — to take what is for many readers the most impressive episode in the *Aeneid* — it is no ordinary abandonment but the origin of the bitter and persistent enmity between Rome and Carthage which culminated finally in the Punic Wars and ended with the burning of Carthage by the Romans. Virgil makes the link with Roman history explicit in the agonized curse of Dido a few moments before her death.

> tum vos, O Tyrii, stirpem et genus omne futurum
> exercete odiis, cinerique haec mittite nostro

---

[6] *A Preface to Paradise Lost* (London, 1942), p. 33.

>   munera. nullus amor populis nex foedera sunto.
>   exoriare aliquis nostris ex ossibus ultor,
>   qui face Dardanios ferroque sequare colonos!
>   4.622–26; cf. 10.11–13

Then do you, O Tyrians, pursue his seed with your hatred for all ages to
come; send this guerdon to our ashes. Let no kindness nor truce be between
the nations. Arise, some avenger, out of our dust, to follow the Dardanian
settlers with firebrand and steel.

The blazing pyre upon which Dido flings herself thus becomes a kind
of grim foreshadowing of the later and larger fire.

There is another implied contrast with Homer in the opening lines
of the *Aeneid*, one which Virgil will elaborate upon in the course of
the epic. In the tenth line, Aeneas is described as *insignem pietate
virum* ("a man excellent in goodness") and, with this phrase, Virgil
introduces a new kind of epic hero. Henceforth, the epithet *pius*
will be as inevitably associated with the name of Aeneas as "fleet of
foot" was with the name of Achilles and "of many counsels" with that
of Odysseus. Unfortunately, there is no single English word which
can adequately convey the full meaning of *pius*. "Good" does well
enough in that the epithet embraces so many different attributes, but,
as Henry Nettleship remarks, the word connotes "not one heroic
quality merely, but the character of the son who loves his father, of
the king who loves his subjects, of the worshipper who reverences
the gods," [7] and who submits, it may be added, dutifully to the de-
mands the gods make upon him, no matter what the cost to him in
personal suffering. Clearly the word *pius* has moral and spiritual
overtones which are lacking in the epithets Homer applies to his
heroes. Here we have an important clue to the central difference
between the Homeric and Virgilian conceptions of heroic virtue.
For Homer, physical courage and prowess were enough. They were
not enough for Virgil, whose hero must display moral courage as
well. He does this chiefly by his willingness to make personal sacri-
fices for a common good. It is the alliance of physical courage with
pietas, and all that *pietas* signifies, which is the distinguishing mark
of the new heroism. So Iloneus describes Aeneas to Dido:

>   rex erat Aeneas nobis, quo iustior alter
>   nec pietate fuit, nec bello maior et armis.
>   1.544–45

Aeneas was our king, foremost of men in righteousness, incomparable in
goodness as in warlike arms.

---

[7] *Lectures and Essays on Subjects Connected with Latin Literature and Scholarship* (Oxford, 1885), p. 104.

One could not ask for a clearer illustration of the difference between the two conceptions than the reactions of Achilles and Aeneas to the main crisis in each of their lives. At the beginning of the *Iliad*, Agamemnon imperiously deprives Achilles of his "meed of honor," the slave girl Briseis, and thereby so lacerates the hero's pride that he retires to his ships, refusing all entreaties to do battle, even when it appears that his inactivity may result in the utter overthrow of the Greek cause. Although Achilles had great provocation, we may doubt whether patriotic Romans would have found much to admire in his display of heroic selfishness.

True, Homer himself is critical of his hero's conduct, but it seems to be equally true that the Greek chieftains understand and to some extent at least sympathize with Achilles' point of view. After all, had not these same chieftains involved themselves in a long and bloody war to salvage the personal honor of Menelaus? Far otherwise is it with Aeneas when he must choose between his love for the Carthaginian queen, Dido, and the patriotic mission to which the gods have dedicated him, the founding of Rome. Virgil had employed all the resources of his art to show the powerful hold which Dido, and the way of life she represents, has over the affections of Aeneas. But when he, too, like Achilles, returns to his ships, it is for a far different purpose.

> at pius Aeneas, quamquam lenire dolentem
> solando cupit et dictis avertere curas,
> multa gemens magnoque animum labefactus amore
> iussa tamen divum exsequitur classemque revisit.
>
> 4.393–96

But good Aeneas, though he would fain soothe and comfort her grief, and quell her passion by speech, with many a sigh, and melted in soul by his great love, yet fulfils the divine commands and returns to his fleet.

As much as the words themselves, the rhythm of these lines, especially of the incomparable third line, taken together with the powerful anticlimactic effect of the listless phrase *classemque revisit*, expresses the nature of Aeneas' personal tragedy. But Rome, and the Roman way of evaluating life, has won a momentous victory.

Virgil's attitude toward the heroic ideal he superseded was complex. For him, as for Romans generally, there was everything to admire in the courage and strength of an Achilles or the genius for wise leadership displayed by an Odysseus. Aeneas, we may note, has in him a good deal of both Achilles and Odysseus. But Virgil could no longer write of war in the same spirit, and with the same attitude, that Homer did. It is largely a question of emphasis. I believe it is

fair to say that the average reader will feel that Homer stresses the
glamour and excitement of war and minimizes its horror, whereas
Virgil stresses the horror and minimizes the glamour. There is, for
example, nothing edifying about the actions of the Greek heroes during the sack of Troy. They gain ingress into Troy through a piece
of shameless treachery and then, in their sack of the city, behave more
like beasts than men. One is compelled to believe, along with Professor Bowra, that Virgil is using the sack of Troy, among other things,
to expose the essential barbarism underlying the old heroic ideal.[8]
This barbarism stands most clearly revealed in the person of Neoptolemus, the son of Achilles.

Neoptolemus possesses many of his father's martial attributes, but
they are unqualified by his father's nobility of spirit. When Achilles
is himself, as he is when near the end of the *Iliad* the aged King
Priam comes to beg the body of his son Hector for burial, he is capable of generous and compassionate action. Neoptolemus, on the other
hand, is as pitiless as a tiger and, like a tiger, he rages through the
halls and corridors of Priam's crumbling palace, slaughtering everyone he meets without regard for age or sex. His savage delight in
killing for the sake of killing does not even balk at sacrilege, and
the culminating atrocity — the murder first of Priam's son and then
of Priam himself — takes place before the very altars of their gods.
The language which Virgil employs to describe this bloody scene
indicates clearly enough his own attitude toward it. Neoptolemus
has just slain Polites before the eyes of his father, and Priam cries
out in anguish:

"Ah, for thy crime, for this thy hardihood, may the gods, if there is goodness
in heaven to care for aught such, pay thee in full thy worthy meed and
return thee the reward that is due! who hast made me look face to face on
my child's murder, and polluted a father's countenance with death. Ah, not
such to a foe was the Achilles whose parentage thou beliest; but he revered
a suppliant's right and trust, restored to the tomb Hector's blood-drained
corpse, and sent me back to my own realm." Thus the old man spoke, and
launched his weak and unwounding spear, which, recoiling straight from the
jarring brass, hung idly from his shield above the boss. Threat Pyrrhus:
"Thou then shalt tell this, and go with the message to my sire the son of Peleus: remember to tell him of my baleful deeds, and the degeneracy of Neoptolemus. Now die." So saying, he drew him quivering to the very altar,
slipping in the pool of his child's blood, and wound his hair in the left hand,
while in the right the sword flashed out and plunged to the hilt in his
side. . . . The great corpse lies along the shore, a head severed from the
shoulders, and a body without a name [2.535–58].

---

[8] *From Virgil to Milton* (London, 1945), pp. 42–43, hereafter cited as Bowra.

The contrast between Neoptolemus and Achilles could not have been made more explicit. The former, we should not neglect to observe, knows well enough how his deed at the altar will be interpreted and brazenly exults in the epithet "degenerate" which he applies to himself in his needlessly cruel mockery of the doomed old man. In Neoptolemus Virgil strips the old heroic ideal of its superficial attractions and lets us see for a moment its sordid underside.

All warriors are not Neoptolemuses and, in his characterization of Turnus, Virgil brings the Homeric ideal back into a steadier focus. More than any other character in the *Aeneid*, Turnus resembles Achilles. In fact, in one place, Virgil calls him another Achilles. The Cumaean Sybil tells Aeneas:

> . . . alius Latio iam partus Achilles
> natus et ipse dea;

> 6.89–90

Another Achilles is already provided in Latium, he too goddess-born.

Professor Bowra has shown how Virgil heightens the comparison between Turnus and Achilles by employing the same similes to describe his hero as Homer had used to describe Achilles.[9] In one respect, however, Turnus is more like Aeneas than Achilles; he is devoted to his country and his people and believes that he is fighting principally for them and only incidentally to win glory for himself. He is, therefore, not without *pietas* but, unlike Aeneas, he is temperamentally incapable of that rigid discipline of the emotional self without which *pietas* cannot reveal itself in wise and good action. In every crisis, his emotions get the better of him; the Achilles in him wins out over the Aeneas. Finally, his pride and immense self-confidence lead him to reject a splendid opportunity for an honorable peace and to commit his own fortunes, and those of his people, to the battlefield, always the court of last authority for men of the Homeric stamp. So blind is his faith in his own strength and courage that he is willing and even eager to oppose them against all the omens and prophecies foretelling his defeat. It is sheer recklessness, sheer *hybris*, and he pays for his pride with his life.

There is a magnificent passage near the end of the poem in which Virgil appears to be summing up in a few lines the old heroic ideal, in all its splendor and greatness and ultimate futility. The time comes for Turnus when, alone and weaponless, he must face the wrath of the oncoming Aeneas. Now there is nothing left him *but* his strength and courage. Seeing a huge stone, *vix illud lecti*

---

[9] Bowra, p. 44.

bis sex cervice subirent (12.899; "scarcely might twelve chosen men lift it on their shoulders"), he lifts it up and hurls it at Aeneas. But this last desperate feat of strength is as unavailing as the ineffectual spear which Priam hurls at Neoptolemus; the stone does not even reach its target. It is the end for Turnus and the heroic ideal he embodies.

This account of the epic tradition, as Homer began it and Virgil changed and embellished it, has been necessarily limited to a discussion of essential points. But perhaps enough has been said to provide a groundwork for what follows. For if, as critics were once fond of saying, Homer made Virgil, it is no less true that Virgil, with the help of Homer, made Milton. He made him in the best sense; that is, he taught him to invent. We have studied the opening lines of the *Aeneid*. Let us now inspect their counterpart in *Paradise Lost*.

Before considering Milton's exordium in detail, however, a few words should be said about its general structure. It begins with a statement of the subject matter of the poem, and this is followed by the invocation to the Muse. Then, at the end of the exordium proper, Milton announces his main theme, the justification of God's ways to Man. Finally, he introduces his narrative by means of a rhetorical question. These are all epic conventions, sanctified by Homeric and Virgilian precedent, but Milton does not use them simply for their prestige value. He is telling his readers something they need to know; that is, he is serving advance notice on them of the particular tradition in which he will be writing his poem and, by implication, inviting the sort of comparison which will lead to a clearer realization of what he himself is contributing to that tradition, or has tried to contribute but failed.

In the order in which he has taken up his conventions, but principally in the spirit in which he has treated them, the main debt is to Virgil. It will be recalled that Virgil's opening lines had two principal objectives: first, to demonstrate that, in scope and substance, his subject was greater than that of either the *Iliad* or the *Odyssey*; and second, to foreshadow a new kind of epic hero. To achieve these objectives as tactfully and modestly as possible, he had consistently and with brilliant success employed the device of the insinuated comparison. Here now are the first nine and a half lines of Milton's exordium:

> Of Man's First Disobedience, and the Fruit
> Of that Forbidden Tree, whose mortal tast
> Brought Death into the World, and all our woe,
> With loss of *Eden*, till one greater Man

> Restore us, and regain the blissful Seat
> Sing Heav'nly Muse, that on the secret top
> Of *Oreb*, or of *Sinai*, didst inspire
> That Shepherd, who first taught the chosen Seed
> In the Beginning how the Heav'ns and Earth
> Rose out of *Chaos*:
>
>   1.1–10

There is, first of all, the apparently innocent phrase at the end of the third line, "and all our woe." Most readers will perceive at once the rhythmical and accentual emphasis Milton has given it, but only a reader familiar with the classical epic will apprehend the reason for that emphasis. The phrase is, in fact, exceedingly guileful; it is a clear reminiscence of a kindred expression occurring in the exordia of all three classical epics. Thus, in the *Iliad*, the wrath of Achilles is responsible for the "woes innumerable" (*muri . . . alge*) of the Greeks. In the *Odyssey*, we learn that the hero will be afflicted by "many woes" (*polla . . . algea*) on his long journey home to Ithaca. Likewise, Aeneas is to undergo "many woes" (*tot . . . casus*) before he can accomplish his divine mission. But, Milton reminds us, Adam's sin of disobedience is the root of *all* our woe. Contrasted with the woes of which he will write — which are those not of a single man or of a single people struggling to be born, but of Man himself — the sufferings described by Homer and Virgil are made to seem relatively petty and unimportant. This is Milton's way of asserting one aspect in which his subject is superior to the epic subjects of the past.

With the phrase "greater Man" he asserts still another aspect in which his subject is superior. The "greater Man" is, of course, Christ, and the primary comparison, as the first line of the poem makes clear, is with Adam. But it is hardly possible that there should not be a secondary allusion to Odysseus or to Aeneas or, more likely still, to both.

Readers will perhaps recall the strategy which Homer — and after Homer, Virgil — used to introduce his hero. This strategy consisted in withholding the name of the hero for many lines after he had been tentatively identified as *that man* (*Od.* 1.3) or simply as *the man* (*Aen.* 1.1). The effect was to produce simultaneously in the minds of readers a kind of suspense and the notion that a hero so incomparable scarcely needed further identification or the author would have provided it. When Milton used the word "Man" in the fourth line of his poem, he could not therefore have been unaware of the inevitable associations it would have had. During the Renaissance, Odysseus and Aeneas were regarded as ideal human types, giving the implicit comparison a propriety it does not have to the same degree for readers today. Nothing could be more fitting than that Milton, in a Christian poem championing Christian ideals of conduct, should invoke a comparison between the noblest representatives of their respective world orders and the supreme exemplar of his. A direct comparison would have been indecorous; so Milton, to overcome the difficulty, adopted the Virgilian tactic of the insinuated comparison. It is a beautiful instance of Miltonic discretion.

This interpretation of the full meaning of Milton's phrase "greater Man" is supported by the verses which follow it. The Heavenly Muse which Milton calls upon is only for a fleeting moment the epic Muse of Homer and Virgil. The rhythmical wave which begins with the first line of the poem reaches its crest with the phrase "Sing Heav'nly Muse," holds there for a moment, and then slowly subsides, and, as it subsides, we see that this Muse is not after all the traditional Muse of classical epic, but the Eternal Voice which spoke to Moses on Mount Horeb and later inspired the Hebrew prophets.

> . . . Or if *Sion* Hill
> Delight thee more, and *Siloa's* Brook that flow'd
> Fast by the Oracle of God; I thence
> Invoke thy aid to my adventrous Song
> That with no middle flight intends to soar
> Above th'*Aonian* Mount, while it pursues
> Things unattempted yet in Prose or Rhime.
>
> 1.10–16

With these verses Milton makes the comparison between the classical and Christian Muse complete in every detail. Siloa's brook, which the Christian Muse haunts and which flows by the Temple of God ("the Oracle") on Mount Sion, is equivalent to the spring haunted by the classical Muses, rising by the altar of Zeus on Helicon, "th'Aonian Mount." In claiming that his song will soar above the Aonian Mount, Milton, of course, is not claiming that he will write a better poem than his illustrious predecessors. He is simply employing the most delicate means available to him as a poet to assert a truth which most readers will accept as indisputable: the superiority of his subject.

This superiority manifests itself in scope as well as subject. To establish the basis for a contrast, Milton follows closely the structural pattern of Virgil's opening lines. Thus, like Virgil, he begins by fixing the temporal limits of his poem. *Paradise Lost* will embrace a period of time stretching from the Fall of Man to the Atonement, a period quite dwarfing the Virgilian time scheme which, the reader will remember, comprehended a period from the time Aeneas and his followers departed from fallen Troy to the building of Rome.

Nothing could be clearer than Milton's indebtedness to Virgil at this point for, in actual fact, the stated limits of both poems turn out to be illusory. The *Aeneid*, chronologically speaking, does not begin with the flight from Troy but with the circumstances which resulted in its destruction, the treachery of Sinon and the gullibility of the Trojans. In the same way, *Paradise Lost* does not chronologically begin with the Fall of Man but with the revolt of Satan. Furthermore, neither poem actually describes the action whereby the final goal is attained — in the case of the *Aeneid*, the founding of Rome, in the case of *Paradise Lost*, the Redemption of Man.

To fill in the historical lacunae, both poems resort to the devices of vision and prophecy. How closely Milton had studied the principles of Virgilian structure is perhaps best illustrated by the way he begins the narrative portion of his poem. He begins it by introducing Satan, the traditional enemy of Man, as Virgil had begun with the mention of Carthage, the traditional enemy of Rome. Then, just as Virgil had accounted for the enmity existing between Rome and Carthage by showing how Juno, motivated by old hatreds, had fostered it, so Milton goes back of the Fall of Man to the revolt of Satan and the motives of envy and revenge which led him to deceive the Mother of mankind. So the building of Carthage, which Virgil describes in the First Book of the *Aeneid*, becomes roughly parallel to the building of Pandemonium in the First Book of *Paradise Lost*. This correspondence is too close to be accidental and is, in fact, confirmed by a remarkable verbal parallel. When, in the First Book of the *Aeneid*, the ships of Aeneas are driven by the storm to seek haven on Carthaginian shores, Aeneas, though himself sick at heart, tries to rally the drooping spirits of his followers. It is the first speech he makes in the poem, and Virgil comments as follows:

> Talia voce refert curisque ingentibus aeger
> spem vultu simulat, premit altum corde dolorem.
> 1.208–9

Such words he utters, and sick with deep distress he feigns hope on his face, and keeps his anguish hidden deep in his breast.

With the very first words he speaks in *Paradise Lost*, Satan tries to revive the sagging courage of his chief lieutenant, Beelzebub, Milton adding:

> So spake th'Apostate Angel, though in pain,
> Vaunting aloud, but rackt with deep despare:
> 1.125–26

And there can be no question that Milton had the Virgilian passage and its context in mind.

Again, in the First Book of the *Aeneid*, Virgil represents Jupiter as prophesying the course of Roman history up to the culminating achievement under Augustus.

> nascetur pulchra Troianus origine Caesar,
> imperium Oceano, famam qui terminet astris,
> Iulius, a magno demissum nomen Iulo.
>
> 1.286–88

From the fair line of Troy a Caesar shall arise, who shall limit his empire with ocean, his glory with the firmament, Julius, inheritor of great Iülus' name.

This is a form of that poetical omniscience which has been termed the principle of reassurance and of which Milton makes constant use in *Paradise Lost* to allay any furtive fears on the part of his readers that Satan may, after all, win out in the end. Then, in the Sixth Book of the *Aeneid*, Anchises leads his son, Aeneas, to a hill (*tumulus*), whence he might see in a vision his descendants generation by generation establishing the greatness of Rome. Milton not only imitates this structural device, he underscores his indebtedness to Virgil by echoing at the appropriate place his very phraseology. After the Archangel Michael, from "a Hill / Of Paradise the highest," has shown Adam a vision of the course of human events from his own time to the Crucifixion and the Ascension, he ends his running commentary with these words — the allusion is to Christ:

> . . . he shall ascend
> The Throne hereditarie, and bound his Reign
> With earths wide bounds, his glory with the Heav'ns.
>
> 12.369–71

And once more, this time by an implied comparison between Christ and Augustus, strategically placed near the end of *Paradise Lost*, Milton reaffirms the transcendent grandeur of his epic idea.

It is often difficult to distinguish between an actual borrowing from another poet and a borrowing which is only apparent because both poets have been drawing from the same wellspring of poetic inspiration and are governed by the same laws of artistic composition. Nevertheless, it is undeniable that, in the exordium of his poem, Milton adopts poetic means similar to those of Virgil to suggest to his readers the vastness of the stage upon which the tragedy of the Fall of Man is to be enacted. Few readers of *Paradise Lost* can have failed to notice how its opening lines are dominated by words and phrases connoting or denoting momentous height, "secret top," "Rose out of *Chaos*," "no middle flight," "soar / Above th'*Aonian* Mount," "upright," "mighty wings," "raise and support," "to the

highth of this great Argument." The effect of this particular colloca-
tion of phrases would appear to be twofold: first, it increases the
effectiveness of the lines which immediately follow, when Milton
writes of the "bottomless perdition" to which Satan and his cohorts
are hurled after their defeat in Heaven; second, the strong upward
tug of movement felt throughout the exordium and culminating in
the phrase "to the highth of this great Argument" communicates a
sense of the almost intolerable strain of the creative effort, helping
to implant in the reader's mind, at the very outset of the undertaking,
a firm conviction of its dignity and importance.

There may have been a time when, as Professor Bowra speculates,
if Milton had written his projected *Arthuriad*, it would have glorified the English people as Virgil's *Aeneid* had glorified the Romans.[10]
Fortunately, Milton abandoned the project, which could only have
resulted in a pallid imitation of the *Aeneid*. Whether the impulse
to abandon it was primarily personal or aesthetic, we do not know.
All we do know is that at the crucial period, the period when he was
actually engaged in the composition of *Paradise Lost*, the wars which
Homer had celebrated to aggrandize the individual and which Virgil had celebrated to aggrandize the state did not, for Milton, foster
a heroism of the highest order. In the Fall of Adam, and its tragic
consequences for mankind, he thought he saw the opportunity to
present the grounds for a nobler, truer heroism than that exhibited
by the epic poetry of the past. "Sad task," he acknowledges,

> . . . yet argument
> Not less but more Heroic than the wrauth
> Of stern *Achilles* on his Foe pursu'd
> Thrice Fugitive about *Troy* Wall; or rage
> Of *Turnus* for *Lavinia* disespous'd,
> Or *Neptun's* ire or *Juno's*, that so long
> Perplex'd the *Greek* and *Cytherea's* Son;
>
> 9.13–19

"Not less but more Heroic." Milton realized, as Virgil had realized,
that to demonstrate the pre-eminence of his own heroic ideal he must
display it in a certain critical relationship with the universally admired heroic ideals embodied in the Homeric poems and the *Aeneid*.
There will be, as we shall see, many important ways in which Milton
will use the materials of classical literature to enrich the content and
meaning of *Paradise Lost*. But, above all, he required Virgil. Without
the *Aeneid*, there could have been no *Paradise Lost* as we know it
today.

---

[10] Bowra, p. 194.

CHAPTER THREE

The Infernal Serpent

Milton was never one to find compromise easy. If the Christian theological tradition had not provided a sufficient sanction for the Promethean Satan we encounter in the first books, *Paradise Lost* might never have been written. Nothing less than such a Satan would do, for, as generations of critics have been saying, to belittle Satan would also be to belittle God. Nor could a story which centered on a contest too patently unequal prove dramatically satisfying. Milton was thus obliged to preserve at least the illusion of equality between the two mighty opposites in his poem. Indeed, to the extent that Satan embodies the principle of evil in the world, to have done otherwise would have been to distort the transparent facts. "Good and evill," Milton writes in the *Areopagitica*, "we know in the field of this World grow up together almost inseparably; and the knowledge of good is so involv'd and interwoven with the knowledge of evill, and in so many cunning resemblances hardly to be discern'd, that those confused seeds which were impos'd on *Psyche* as an incessant labour to cull out, and sort asunder, were not more intermixt."[1] The moralist who wrote those words, who had earlier given us Comus, and in *Paradise Lost* was to give us the double-formed Sin in the image of her maker, would be no more likely to underplay the superficial attractions of evil than he would its frightful destructive powers.

Without doubt Milton's portrait of the early Satan was also influenced by the grand design he had worked out for his poem. He urgently needed a figure interesting enough to engage our attention until by slow gradation it could be diverted to his principals, Adam and Eve. By the middle of the Tenth Book, the shift has been completed, our interest by this time is wholly focused on Adam and Eve and their precarious predicament, and Satan is accordingly allowed to drop out of sight. Professor E. E. Stoll has made this point so well that I shall quote him directly:

. . . since, by the premise, man is innocent, ignorant, sinless, inexperienced, only eight days old, and since by tradition as well as necessity the action

---

[1] "Areopagitica" in *Works*, IV, 310.

is wholly in the hands of the Tempter, why, the Tempter, then, must, until after the Fall, fill the scene. Also he must do that on his own account as intrinsically far more interesting . . . just as both Adam and Eve are far more interesting and appealing at and after the Fall than before, and Eve (the bigger sinner) than her husband. Then, with them, too, wickedness puts goodness to the test and gives the real virtues a chance of proving their mettle.[2]

The gradual shift of interest from Satan to Adam and Eve begins when the human pair shows the first symptoms of frailty. But Stoll is right. They do not truly "fill the scene" until the Fall takes place. Someone must bear the burden in the interval, and Satan was not only the logical choice, he was the only possible one.

We must not overlook, however, yet another reason for the kind of Satan we get in the early books, a reason no less compelling than those which have already been given. In the preceding chapter, I tried to suggest how completely Milton understood the implications of the classical epic, how in effect they served to point out to him the direction which his own epic must take if its contribution to the tradition was to have a permanent significance. Here Satan could be made to perform an invaluable function. For criticizing the brand of heroism which the life and death of Christ had relegated to a position of the second order, what more telling device was available to Milton than to embody the old heroism in Satan and then to discredit it by exposing its deficiencies and inadequacies? And, after all, had not Virgil pointed the way in his treatment of Turnus? The readers who have thrilled to the valorous words and action of the early Satan, who have been unable to withhold from him their admiration for his indomitable spirit, have not been deceiving themselves. The virtues they see in him are not the illusory product of romantic imaginings. They are there and designedly there. It is as futile to deny their presence as it is to try to make out Satan to be the hero of the poem. That the heroic Satan of the early books reflects Milton's active intention and is not, as some critics have argued, a subtle perversion of it should be indisputable on the evidence of the strategy he employs at the very outset.

Milton begins his poem at a point in time soon after the defeat and rout of the Fallen Angels. This immediately put at his disposal a flourishing theological tradition. According to this tradition, since Satan was created by God, the wickedness of his nature could not possibly have derived from Creation, but from a progressive corruption of the will. By beginning at the point he does, Milton was well

---

[2] "Postscript to 'Give the Devil His Due,' " *PQ*, XXVIII (1949), 175.

within his rights in dramatizing those Promethean qualities in Satan which he knew were essential to his poem. Before Pride had brought about his Fall, Satan had been one of the greatest of the Archangels [3] and, as we first see him, he still retains much of his pristine grandeur and magnificence.

> . . . his form had yet not lost
> All her Original brightness, nor appear'd
> Less than Arch Angel ruind, and th'excess
> Of Glory obscur'd:

> 1.591–94

This splendor receives an added emphasis from the fact that it is set against the flattering background of Hell. On Satan's side, too, is the reader's own instinctive sympathy for the underdog, the fact that he has not yet been exposed in a dramatic context to any other point of view, and above all perhaps the seductive character of the poetry Milton has put into Satan's mouth. These factors work inexorably together to produce an image in our minds of a figure only slightly less than godlike in its heroic proportions. We may have reservations (and Mr. Lewis has carefully explained to us what they should be) [4] but the ineluctable fact is that only in retrospect do our second thoughts about Satan assume their undeniable importance. And, even then, they do not seriously weaken our first impression of Satan; they succeed only in qualifying it. The figure in its main outlines remains unblurred.

With respect to Milton's intention in depicting Satan as he does, we surely ought not to ignore the further evidence of a passage in the Eleventh Book. It comes in the form of a comment on the Giants of Genesis.

> Such were these Giants, men of high renown;
> For in those dayes Might onely shall be admir'd,
> And Valour and Heroic Vertu call'd;
> To overcome in Battle, and subdue
> Nations, and bring home spoils with infinite
> Man-slaughter, shall be held the highest pitch
> Of human Glorie, and for Glorie done
> Of triumph, to be styl'd great Conquerours,
> Patrons of Mankind, Gods, and Sons of Gods,
> Destroyers rightlier call'd and Plagues of men.
> Thus Fame shall be atchiev'd, renown on Earth,
> And what most merits fame in silence hid.

> 11.688–99

---

[3] See *P.L.* 5.659–61.
[4] *Preface*, pp. 93 ff.

What Milton says about the Giants is hardly justified by the account of them we find in Genesis, which is brief and noncommittal. "There were giants in the earth in those days; and also after that, when the sons of God came in unto the daughters of men, and they bare children to them, the same became mighty men which were of old, men of renown" (6.4). On the other hand, his remarks are exactly applicable to the code of the Homeric heroes. They are also applicable to Satan and his followers. Indeed, the line "Destroyers rightlier call'd and Plagues of men" recalls both the fact that one name for Satan is the Destroyer and the fine simile in the First Book, where the Fallen Angels are compared with the plague of locusts which descended upon Egypt in her evil day (1.338–43).

"In those days," Milton proclaims, "Might onely shall be admir'd." The principle of might, therefore, he embodies in Satan and, along with might, the two motifs in the old heroic creed which made it so destructive — pride, manifesting itself in an insatiable desire for personal glory and renown, and death-defying valor. In the preceding chapter, I quoted at length from Sarpedon's speech to Glaukos in the *Twelfth Iliad* because it seemed to provide in narrow compass the most perfect expression of the Homeric conception of heroism. Long ago Lord Monboddo called attention to the resemblance between this speech and Satan's when the latter offers to venture forth into the unknown in an attempt to locate Paradise.[5]

> But I should ill become this Throne, O Peers,
> And this Imperial Sov'ranty, adorn'd
> With splendor, arm'd with power, if aught propos'd
> And judg'd of public moment, in the shape
> Of difficulty or danger could deterr
> Me from attempting. Wherefore do I assume
> These Royalties, and not refuse to Reign,
> Refusing to accept as great a share
> Of hazard as of honour, due alike
> To him who Reigns, and so much to him due
> Of hazard more, as he above the rest
> High honourd sits?

2.445–56

So Sarpedon had defined the principle of *noblesse oblige* to Glaukos as the two friends made ready to hurl themselves on the enemy. Satan's speech has all the ringing accents of the old heroism and makes the same assumptions. Grudging indeed we would be if we

---

[5] For Sarpedon's speech, see above, p. 24. Lord Monboddo's note is quoted by H. J. Todd, *P.L.* 2.445, in his edition of Milton's *Poetical Works* (6 vols., London, 1801), hereafter cited as Todd. Vols. II and III contain *Paradise Lost*.

could not find it in our hearts to admire Satan for the leadership and courage he displays on this and other occasions. We must give, as Professor Stoll says, the devil his due.

But we are doing Milton a disservice if we leave it at that. The Sarpedon parallel works by contrast as well as by comparison, and, to avoid a distortion of the total picture, equal consideration must be given to both sets of derived meanings. The noble end to which the courage of Sarpedon is directed calls attention to, and heavily underscores, the vile purpose which animates Satan — the diminution of God's glory through the destruction of mankind. This is a first point. Another is suggested by Lord Monboddo's comment on the oratorical style of Satan's speech. Milton, he says, "has given it so much of the rhetorical cast, and dressed it so up with sentences and enthymemas, after the manner of Demosthenes, who, as I have said elsewhere, was his model for speeches, that Homer is hardly to be found in it." The rhetorical effects in the speech are, of course, accounted for by its dramatic context; Satan is actually delivering an oration to his troops. Nevertheless, the contrast between the simple, impassioned eloquence of Sarpedon and Satan's artful eloquence calls the latter's sincerity into question. The "sentences and enthymemas" with which Satan has tricked out his speech must surely have been purposeful on the part of the poet. They help illuminate Satan's real motive for venturing forth alone.

This interesting parallel furnishes a good example of how one kind of association is likely to function in the poem. Obviously, Milton could not risk open allusions to the epic heroes of antiquity without violating decorum. What he could do, however, he did; that is, he builds up a cluster of associations around Satan and his followers which exert a steady pressure upon his readers, inviting them, almost compelling them, time after time to make specific acts of comparison and contrast. The covert allusion has never been applied to a more telling advantage. It does Milton yeoman service in helping to cultivate in his reader the strenuously ambivalent feelings about Satan which are essential to a proper understanding of the poem. Thus, if the implied comparisons with Achilles, Turnus, Odysseus, Aeneas, Prometheus, and other heroes serve to magnify our impression of Satan's heroic grandeur, they also simultaneously provide the grounds for impugning him both as character and symbol. And it seems likely that they may often have an anticipatory function as well. Let me illustrate.

One of the most magnificent visual images in the whole of *Para-*

dise Lost occurs right after the roll call of the Fallen Angels in the First Book. "Thir visages and stature as of Gods," these angels stand now before Satan in battle array, awaiting his command.

> . . . he above the rest
> In shape and gesture proudly eminent
> Stood like a Towr; his form had yet not lost
> All her Original brightness, nor appear'd
> Less than Arch Angel ruind, and th'excess
> Of Glory obscur'd: As when the Sun new ris'n
> Looks through the Horizontal misty Air
> Shorn of his Beams, or from behind the Moon
> In dim Eclips disastrous twilight sheds
> On half the Nations, and with fear of change
> Perplexes Monarchs. Dark'n'd so, yet shon
> Above them all th'Arch Angel:
>
> 1.589–600

The beautiful passage moved Dr. Newton to the following rapturous tribute: "What a noble description is here of Satan's person! . . . The greatest masters in painting had not such sublime ideas as Milton, and among all their Devils have drawn no portrait comparable to this."[6] I do not think it has been noticed that Milton's cluster of images has for its point of departure a passage in the *Aeneid* describing Turnus in the midst of his troops.

> . . . ipse inter primos praestanti corpore Turnus
> vertitur arma tenens et toto vertice supra est.
>
> 7.783–84

Himself too among the foremost, splendid in beauty of body, Turnus moves armed and towers a whole head over all.

A verbal and structural likeness to the first unit of Milton's description which is too close to be coincidental proclaims Milton's indebtedness. Also it seems probable that Virgil's second line suggested the simile "Stood like a Towr." If there are remaining doubts, they should vanish without a trace when it is pointed out that the lines describing Turnus also follow an extended roll call, in this case of his Ausonian captains.[7]

The initial effect of associating Satan with the powerful literary memories of Turnus' strength and beauty would be to render Satan's physical presence more glorious than ever. But is this all the allusion

---

[6] *Paradise Lost. A Poem in Twelve Books. The Second Edition, with Notes of Various Authors, by Thomas Newton, D.D.* (2 vols., London, 1750). See the note to 1.589.

[7] Editors usually cite Homer's more famous catalogue of the Greek ships in the *Second Iliad* as the inspiration for Milton's roll call of the demons. So it may ultimately have been, but the allusion to Turnus indicates that, as usual, Milton had Virgil immediately in mind.

might be supposed to do? Are we not in addition to think of the false standards to which all that strength and beauty were so irrevocably committed, of Turnus as the embodiment of a way of life and mode of thinking which were outworn and dying? The extension of the comparison in the reader's mind to include this chastening reflection would not only imply by analogy the deficiencies of the code to which Satan himself subscribes but would also serve to reassure the reader of his certain defeat in the end. Later I shall offer other evidence for believing that this allusion was no isolated phenomenon but part of Milton's grand strategy for the covert discrediting of Satan.

Now, as we know, Turnus is the specific means Virgil adopts to criticize the standards of Achilles. Everyone will have noticed the resemblances between the great hero of the *Iliad* and Satan. Like Satan, Achilles defies a central authority and from basically the same impulse, "a sense of injur'd merit." Both are motivated by revenge. Both are proud, disdainful, envious, and egregiously self-centered. Above all else, both passionately seek to win glory for themselves and "renown on Earth." But these similarities must not be pushed too hard or they will distort our perspective. Achilles and Satan share many qualities, many motives, but in the latter they are heightened to such a degree that to indulge in easy comparisons is likely to be misleading. Thus, the desire of Achilles for revenge is frightening in its intensity and in the havoc it causes but, in view of the standards prevalent at the time, particularly the emphasis upon personal honor, there is nothing depraved about it. We cannot say the same for Satan's desire for revenge. His is monstrous, both because of the circumstances which have given rise to it and the innocence of those who must suffer to gratify it. Furthermore, Achilles learns something. That must be the significance of the episode near the end of the poem when Achilles, his blood lust quenched, graciously permits King Priam's request to be allowed to give his son Hector the honorable burial which that age prized so much. His behavior on this occasion is in marked contrast to earlier attitudes. If, on the other hand, Satan at first learns anything, his terrible pride will not permit him to profit from it.

The contrast, emphasizing Satan's blind intransigence, is brilliantly exploited in a passage familiar to every reader. Satan, just off the Burning Lake, addresses Beelzebub.

> Here we may reign secure, and in my choyce
> To reign is worth ambition though in Hell:
> Better to reign in Hell, then serve in Heav'n.
>
> 1.261–63

Noble words indeed, reflecting, as scholars tell us, the great doctrine of the supremacy of mind over matter. Editors cite parallels from Aeschylus and Phineas Fletcher, but the allusion also glances at Achilles' disillusioned answer to Odysseus after the latter, encountering Achilles in Hades, had hailed him as "a great prince here among the dead." The answer:

Nay, speak not comfortably to me of death, oh great Odysseus. Rather would I live on ground as the hireling of another, with a landless man who had no great livelihood, than bear sway among all the dead that be departed [*Odyssey*, p. 176].

Here the contrast hurts Satan, and hurts him badly. Hades had humbled the once-proud Achilles almost beyond recognition, but Hell had only served to harden Satan in his ambition. Nothing could more clearly set off the towering and uncompromising pride of Satan, determined to rule at all costs, to be first in everything, even in Hell, even — one does not hesitate to add — in suffering.

The covert allusions I have been discussing are in no sense atypical. Examples could easily be multiplied. My concern, however, is not with number but with method and purpose. For the sheer bulk of these allusions, the reader is referred to the annotated editions of *Paradise Lost*, especially those of Newton and Todd. He will find, and it should occasion no surprise, that this kind of allusion occurs most frequently in the first four books.[8] By the beginning of the Fifth Book, our growing suspicions have been confirmed. Satan's conduct has opened our eyes wide to his real nature and also to the fact that even this nature is undergoing a slow but inexorable defilement. The work of the camouflaged allusions has therefore largely been done. One does not need to insinuate physical and moral inadequacies which are plainly evident. The first crucial test for Satan has come and gone. This test occurs when, at the end of the Fourth Book, he meets the Archangel Gabriel face to face. It is then that he and the values he represents are, quite literally, weighed in the balance and found wanting. To this episode I now turn.

The episode begins with a reminiscence of the capture and scornful questioning of the spy Dolon by Odysseus and Diomedes.[9] Ithuriel and Zephon apprehend Satan "Squat like a Toad, close at the eare of *Eve*" and convey him into the presence of their leader Gabriel. Satan and Gabriel exchange angry words and only the hanging forth of God's golden scales averts a single combat between the two cham-

---

[8] And in the first half of the Sixth Book, which describes the War in Heaven. This war, of course, antedates the events described in the first four books.

[9] *Iliad*, pp. 176 ff. And see Upton's note, quoted by Todd, *P.L.* 4.866.

pions. The scales measure Satan's chances in such a combat; one weight symbolizes the consequences of staying and fighting, the other of withdrawal. The former kicks the beam and Gabriel, correctly interpreting the evidence, says to Satan:

> Satan, I know thy strength, and thou knowst mine,
> Neither our own but giv'n; what follie then
> To boast what Arms can doe, since thine no more
> Than Heav'n permits, nor mine, though doubld now
> To trample thee as mire: for proof look up,
> And read thy Lot in yon celestial Sign
> Where thou are weigh'd, and shown how light, how weak,
> If thou resist.

4.1006–13

No reader could fail to catch the echo of the Book of Daniel and to perceive its significance in this place. "Thou art weighed in the balances and art found wanting" (5.27). This was the judgment of God against the proud and presumptuous Belshazzar, King of Babylon. The golden scales correspond to the handwriting on the wall. Seeing them, Satan knows that God has spoken and he flees without a word. This is the episode in its broad outlines. It will repay a closer analysis.

The golden scales which God suspends in the heavens to prejudge Satan are borrowed from classical literature. In the *Eighth Iliad*, Homer tells how Zeus balanced his golden scales and "put therein two fates of death," one for the Greeks and one for the Trojans, and weighed them. He repeats the motif in the *Twenty-second Iliad* under similar circumstances, this time to indicate the outcome of the duel between Hector and Achilles. So struck, apparently, was Virgil with the device that he imitated it in his description of the single combat between Aeneas and Turnus. Milton remembered all three of these accounts, but it is again the Virgilian influence which is paramount.

There is no descriptive prelude to the battle between Hector and Achilles. Before Aeneas and Turnus come to blows, however, the former is described as clashing his armor horribly.

> quantus Athos aut quantus Eryx aut ipse coruscis
> cum fremit ilicibus quantus gaudetque nivali
> vertice se attollens pater Appenninus ad auras.[10]

12.701–3

Vast as Athos, or as Eryx, or as the lord of Apennine when he roars with his tossing ilex woods and rears his snowy crest rejoicing into air.

---

[10] In the *Thirteenth Iliad* Homer had compared Hector to a snow-clad peak but he does not identify it. It is altogether typical of Virgil that, in remembering the simile and adapting it, he should furnish it with a local habitation and a name.

Another simile marks the moment when the battle is actually joined.

> ac velut ingenti Sila summove Taburno
> cum duo conversis inimica in proelia tauri
> frontibus incurrunt, pavidi cessere magistri,
> stat pecus omne metu mutum, mussantque iuvencae
> quis nemori imperitet, quem tota armenta sequantur;
> . . . .
> non aliter Tros Aeneas et Daunius heros
> concurrunt clipeis; ingens fragor aethera complet.

12.715–19, 723–24

And as in broad Sila or high on Taburnus, when two bulls rush to deadly battle forehead to forehead, the herdsmen retire in terror, all the cattle stand dumb in dismay, and the heifers murmur in doubt which shall be lord in the woodland, which the whole herd must follow . . . even thus Aeneas of Troy and the Daunian hero rush together shield to shield; the mighty crash fills the sky.

Milton adapts both similes with some significant changes. While Satan and Gabriel are exchanging their high and angry words, the angels begin forming a half-circle about their leader:

> With ported Spears, as thick as when a field
> Of *Ceres* ripe for harvest waving bends
> Her bearded Grove of ears, which way the wind
> Swayes them; the careful Plowman doubting stands
> Least on the threshing floore his hopeful sheaves
> Prove chaff.

4.980–85

Milton has changed the terms of the comparison, motivated doubtless by a concern for decorum, and at the same time has supplied them with a greater visual force. Shafts of wheat are exactly right for the "ported Spears." The "careful" and "doubting" plowman is likewise a decorous substitution for the cattle which stand "dumb in dismay" (*metu mutum*) and the heifers who "murmur in doubt" (*mussant*, followed by the dubitative subjunctive). There is reason for the fears which the simile is obviously designed to promote in the reader, for opposed to Gabriel,

> On th'other side *Satan* allarm'd
> Collecting all his might dilated stood,
> Like *Teneriff* or *Atlas* unremov'd:
> His stature reacht the Skie, and on his Crest
> Sat horror Plum'd;

4.985–89

A formidable figure, which loses none of its formidability by the implied comparison with Aeneas. We observe that Virgil's mountains are dwarfed by Milton's, and that, whereas Virgil's "lord of the Apennine," to which Aeneas' stature is compared, merely rears his crest far into the air, Satan's stature actually "reacht the Skie" — the reader quickly gets the idea. But Milton, not content with the allusion to Aeneas, adds a detail to his description of Satan which also involves Turnus in the comparison. The vivid abstraction, "and on his Crest / Sat horror Plum'd" distils the essence of Virgil's striking image of the horrible, snakelike Chimaera, "breathing from her throat Aetnean flames," which adorned the crest of Turnus' helmet.[11]

At this point God intervenes, the golden scales are hung in the sky, and Satan learns the meaning of fear.

> . . . The Fiend lookt up and knew
> His mounted scale aloft: nor more; but fled
> Murmuring, and with him fled the shades of night.
>
> 4.1013–15

With these lines the Fourth Book ends, and with them ends any dream Satan may have entertained of resorting to armed force in his irreconcilable war with God. Is it chance, therefore, that Milton, at this particular time and place in his story, saw fit to end the Fourth Book with a final allusion to Turnus? For the last verse of the book is a skillful reworking of the last line of the *Aeneid* which, briefly, poignantly, and unforgettably, records the death of Turnus and the passage of his soul to the eternal shades, *vitaque cum gemitu fugit indignata sub umbras* ("and the life with a moan flies indignant into the dark").[12] The death of Turnus, as we have seen, did not have its complete meaning in itself. With him perished a whole creed, a whole outlook on life. Satan does not perish, but it is not only he who has been weighed in the balance and been found wanting. It is his code, the heroic values he incorporates, the principle of "what Arms can doe." Henceforth he will forgo the methods of Achilles and Turnus and resort to guile, the method of Odysseus. There is no other course open to him.

What does all this mean? Why, for example, is Milton so concerned to forge such powerful links between Satan and Turnus? The most plausible answer is that he hopes, by so doing, his readers will more readily perceive the fact that Satan and Turnus perform similar functions. Once they have perceived and acknowledged this, other important relations will begin to form into a pattern. For Turnus,

---

[11] *Aen.* 7.785–86: *cui triplici crinita iuba galea alta Chimaeram / sustinet Aetnaeos efflantem faucibus ignis.* The two lines which directly precede these have been quoted above, p. 45, in another connection. It is clear that Milton had the passage very much in mind.

[12] Cf. Milton's "fled / Murmuring" with the phrase *cum gemitu fugit* and his "shades of night" with Virgil's *sub umbras. Umbrae* are literally "shades" or "shadows."

it can scarcely be denied, stands in the same relationship to Aeneas as Satan to the Fallen Adam. Just as Aeneas embodies the Roman *virtus* and *pietas* which Virgil would set up in the place of the discredited military virtues of an earlier age, so the Fallen Adam comes eventually to exemplify the Christian ideal of conduct which for Milton constituted the only true heroism — a heroism which Adam himself defines just before he leaves the Garden of Eden forever.

> Henceforth I learne, that to obey is best,
> And love with fear the onely God, to walk
> As in his presence, ever to observe
> His providence, and on him sole depend,
> Mercifull over all his works, with good
> Still overcoming evil, and by small
> Accomplishing great things, by things deemd weak
> Subverting worldly strong, and worldly wise
> By simply meek; that suffering for Truths sake
> Is fortitude to highest victorie,
> And to the faithful Death the Gate of Life;
> Taught this by his example whom I now
> Acknowledge my Redeemer ever blest.
>
> 12.561–73

This it is which "most merits fame," as opposed to "renown on Earth," and if the one is represented by Adam, the other is represented by Satan.

Milton follows the Virgilian pattern as scrupulously as his subject matter will allow. He invests Satan with a might far greater than that of Achilles and a guile far more subtle than that of Odysseus.[13] So endowed, Satan begins his assault upon mankind. With the Fall, he wins a temporary victory, but the Fall is merely the prelude to the more crucial conflict which follows. This conflict, as befits the issues involved, does not take place on a battlefield like the mortal struggle between Turnus and Aeneas, but is fought out in the arena of Adam's moral being. It is there, at the end of the Tenth Book, that Satan is finally and permanently repulsed when Adam humbles himself before God and with contrite heart submits to His will.

With this victory, which is no less decisive than the victory of Aeneas over Turnus, Milton has succeeded in illustrating his moral by an inversion of the heroic scale of values. He has demonstrated that out of the very weakness of man can emerge a spiritual strength sufficient, with God's help, to defeat all the mighty purposes of Satan. This is a central Christian paradox and, for it, Milton is indebted

---

[13] It is surely unnecessary to specify the occasions when Satan reminds us of Odysseus. Professor Bowra singles out the deception Satan practiced upon Uriel (3.613 ff.) as being especially reminiscent.

only to the theological tradition which formulated it. But in effectively translating that paradox into the concrete terms of the epic,
Milton learned much that was valuable from Virgil and, throughout,
has constantly drawn upon Homer as well as Virgil to enrich and
expand his meanings. He might have succeeded without them, but
it is hard to see how he could have succeeded so well.

Satan could not be made to illustrate the deficiencies of the old
concept of "Heroick virtue" without possessing the qualities which
exemplified it. So far I have been dealing with a class of allusion
which, in the aesthetic sense, does Satan more good than harm. The
comparisons with the epic heroes of the past deepen, rather than
diminish, our impression of Satan's transcendent grandeur, make him
not less but more heroic in weak mortal eyes. There was a real problem for Milton here. The more successful he was in promoting the
impression of Satan's greatness, the more difficult he would find it to
win the reader's assent to his degradation. The first impression might
well prove too powerful to be dislodged. And that, as every student of
Milton knows, has been precisely the experience of many readers,
among them eminent critics whose judgment in such matters we have
no warrant to dismiss lightly.

The most recent, and in some respects the most cogent, of these
critics has been Arthur J. A. Waldock. Commenting on Satan's soliloquy at the beginning of the Fourth Book, he says flatly: "This is a
Satan that we have not felt before, nor even dimly felt." Or, again of
the same soliloquy: "The Satan of the Address to the Sun is not a
development from the old, he is not a changed Satan, he is a *new*
Satan." [14] It is hardly possible to overestimate the seriousness of this
charge. If Professor Waldock is right, it must be conceded that *Paradise Lost* suffers from a grave flaw. I cannot, of course, within the
limits I have prescribed for myself in this study, take up the charge
in detail. But against the theory that there are really two Satans in
the poem, I should like to cite the evidence of another class of allusion.

The image patterns I am about to explore are those in which the
theme of monstrosity is adumbrated. Since Professor Waldock finds
the new Satan making his debut on Mount Niphates — that is, at
the very beginning of the Fourth Book — I will limit my discussion
to the first three books. In these books there are two kinds of veiled
allusion which perform the task of systematic disparagement, allusions to the deformed giants who warred on Jove and allusions to
serpents or dragons. Both kinds are at work the very first time we

---

[14] *Paradise Lost and Its Critics* (Cambridge, Eng., 1947), pp. 86, 82.

really see Satan in the poem. This is the well-known passage in which
he is described as lying half-submerged on the Burning Lake,

> With Head up-lift above the wave, and Eyes
> That sparkling blaz'd, his other Parts besides
> Prone on the Flood, extended long and large
> Lay floating many a rood, in bulk as huge
> As whom the Fables name of monstrous size,
> *Titanian,* or *Earth-born,* that warr'd on *Jove,*
> *Briareos* or *Typhon,* whom the Den
> By ancient *Tarsus* held, or that Sea-beast
> *Leviathan,*

                                        1.193–201

For the first two and a half lines of his description Milton is indebted to a passage in the Second Book of the *Aeneid.* Aeneas has
just been telling Dido how the priest Laocoon and his two children
were crushed to death by monstrous sea serpents, an omen presaging
the Fall of Troy. He recalls the terror of the beholders as they saw
the serpents cleaving their way through the waters to the shore, where
Laocoon was slaying a sacrificial bull at the altars of Neptune.

> ecce autem gemini a Tenedo tranquilla per alta,
> horresco referens, immensis orbibus angues
> incumbunt pelago pariterque ad litora tendunt;
> pectora quorum inter fluctus arrecta iubaeque
> sanguineae superant undas; pars cetera pontum
> pone legit sinuatque immensa volumine terga.
> fit sonitus spumate salo; iamque arva tenebant
> ardentisque oculos suffecti sanguine et igni
> sibila lambebant linguis vibrantibus ora.
> diffugimus visu exsangues.

                                        2.203–12

And lo! from Tenedos, over the placid depths (I shudder as I recall) two
snakes in enormous coils press down the sea and advance together to the
shore; their breasts rise through the surge, and their blood-red crests overtop
the waves; the rest trails through the main behind and wreathes back in
voluminous curves; the brine gurgles and foams. And now they gained
the fields, while their bloodshot eyes blazed with fire and their tongues
lapped and flickered in their hissing mouths. We scatter, blanched at the
sight.

Few poets have so successfully evoked an atmosphere of fascinated
horror. And, perhaps more than anything else, it was this atmosphere
which Milton wished to absorb into his own lines describing Satan
on the Burning Lake, first as he lay there prostrate and then as he
made his way to shore. The only difference between the phrase "up-
lift above the wave" and Virgil's *inter fluctus arrecta* (1.206) is that
the one is applied to Satan's head, the other to the breasts of the ser-

pents (cf. the closely parallel phrase *iubaeque / sanguineae superant undas*). Again, the expression "Eyes / That sparkling blaz'd" virtually translates Virgil's *ardentisque oculos suffecti . . . igni* (1.210). [15] To continue, the lines

> . . . his other Parts besides
> Prone on the Flood, extended long and large
> Lay floating many a rood,
>
> 1.194–96

have their verbal and structural counterpart in Virgil's

> . . . pars cetera pontum
> pone legit sinuatque immensa volumine terga.[16]
>
> 2.207–8

Finally, as Virgil had done, Milton contrives the same effect of a menacing movement toward the shore, accompanied by a violent agitation of the elements.

> Forthwith upright he rears from off the Pool
> His mighty Stature; on each hand the flames
> Drivn backward slope thir pointing spires, and rowld
> In billows, leave i' th' midst a horrid Vale.
> Then with expanded wings he stears his flight
> Aloft, incumbent on the dusky Air
> That felt unusual weight, till on dry Land
> He lights,
>
> 1.221–28

The resemblance here is quite general, but one of Milton's phrases constitutes the kind of clue which delights the heart of the literary detective. Virgil uses the expression *incumbunt pelago* ("press down the sea") to describe the way in which the sea serpents swim toward the doomed Laocoon. Milton has "incumbent on the dusky Air." He is clearly using the word in its etymological sense, "pressing down upon." According to the *O.E.D.*, the first appearance of the word with this meaning is found in Sir Henry Wotton's *Elements of Architecture*, printed in 1624. The next listed occurrence is from the passage in *Paradise Lost*. Under these linguistic circumstances, and in view of the fact that only a few lines earlier it is reasonably certain that Milton was alluding to the Laocoon story, I do not hesitate to suggest

---

[15] This would help to explain, if not to justify, a tautology which irritated Mr. Eliot. Of this phrase, he writes: "I am not too happy about eyes that both blaze and sparkle, unless Milton meant us to imagine a roaring fire ejecting sparks: and that is *too* fiery an image for even supernatural eyes." "Milton" (1947), reprinted from *The Proceedings of the British Academy*, Vol. XXXIII, in *Milton Criticism: Selections from Four Centuries*, ed. James Thorpe (London, 1951), p. 327.

[16] Was the phrase *sinuatque immensa volumine terga* in Milton's view when later (2.651–52) he refers to Sin's serpentine nether parts as being "Voluminous and vast"?

that Milton was still thinking of Virgil's serpents, and wanted his readers to think of them, when he composed the lines I have just quoted.

Nevertheless, the major debt of the passage is to a source much closer to hand, Spenser's *Faerie Queene*. Here is the pertinent stanza.

> Then, with his waving wings displayed wyde,
> Himselfe up high he lifted from the ground,
> And with strong flight did forcibly divyde
> The yielding ayre, which nigh too feeble found
> Her flitting parts, and element unsound,
> To beare so great a weight: he, cutting way
> With his broad sayles, about him soared round;
> At last, low stouping with unweldy sway,
> Snatcht up both horse and man, to beare them quite away.[17]
>
> 1.11.18

Milton seems fully as much indebted to the structure of Spenser's lines as he is to their substance.

> Spenser: Then, with his waving wings displayed
> Milton: Then with expanded wings
> Spenser: Himselfe up high he lifted from the ground,
> Milton: Forthwith upright he rears from off the Pool
> Spenser: To beare so great a weight:
> Milton: That felt unusual weight,

The force of these borrowings from Spenser may hardly be said to contradict the central metaphorical tendency of the passage in which they appear. Many readers will already have recognized the context from which Spenser's stanza has been taken. He is describing the initial assault of the Dragon upon the Red Cross Knight.

This well-known episode, with its fine descriptive effects and transparent Christian allegory, was clearly made to order for Milton's purposes. In exploiting it, here and elsewhere in the poem, Milton sets himself in a relation with Spenser strikingly reminiscent of that of Virgil with Homer or Ennius. The verbal echoes of Spenser are seldom an end in themselves; they are employed on graver business. A case in point, and a particularly instructive one, is the systematic use to which Milton puts his allusions to Spenser's allegorical Dragon. These are scattered throughout the poem and it is probably on this account that their collective function has not been clearly perceived. One such allusion has just been cited. Another occurs in the Second

---

[17] By design or coincidence the hawking metaphor ("low stouping"), here applied to the Dragon, is applied by Milton to Satan when, after his long journey through Chaos, he at length comes to "stoop" (3.73) on "the bare outside of this World." Quotations from the *Faerie Queene* are taken from the Cambridge edition of the *Complete Poetical Works*, edited by R. E. Neil Dodge (Boston, 1936).

Book when Milton is describing the difficulties Satan encounters in
negotiating Chaos.

> . . . nigh founderd on he fares,
> Treading the crude consistence, half on foot,
> Half flying; behoves him now both Oare and Saile.
>
> 2.940–42

Spenser, too, likens the flight of the Dragon to the movement of a
ship.

> His flaggy winges, when forth he did display,
> Were like two sayles, in which the hollow wynd
> Is gathered full, and worketh speedy way:
> And eke the pennes, that did his pineons bynd,
> Were like mayne-yardes, with flying canvas lynd,
>
> 1.11.10

Editors draw the parallel tight by comparing the phrase Milton applies to Satan, "half on foot, / Half flying," to Spenser's description
of the Dragon as "halfe flying and halfe footing" in its haste to attack
the Red Cross Knight. One may add that, in general, throughout the
whole of the voyage through Chaos, Satan flies in a manner much
more reminiscent of Spenser's heavy-bodied dragon than of any of
God's angels.

Another allusion of this kind appears in the Sixth Book. It is based
upon an association with the Dragon at the moment it received its
deathblow at the hands of the Knight.

> So downe he fell, and forth his life did breth,
> That vanisht into smoke and cloudes swift;
> So downe he fell, that th'earth him underneath
> Did grone, as feeble so great load to lift;
> So downe he fell, as an huge rocky clift,
> Whose false foundacion waves have washt away,
> With dreadfull poyse is from the mayne-land rift,
> And, rolling downe, great Neptune doth dismay;
> So downe he fell, and like an heaped mountaine lay.
>
> 1.11.54

Is it strange that Milton should have thought of adapting Spenser's
fine simile to his description of how Satan reeled from the mighty
sword stroke of Abdiel just before the angelic armies clash in the
heavens? Although Milton has improved upon Spenser's figure, there
can be little doubt that it provides the foundation upon which he
builds.

> . . . ten paces huge
> He back recoild; the tenth on bended knee
> His massie Spear upstaid; as if on Earth

> Winds under ground or waters forcing way
> Sidelong, had push't a Mountain from his seat
> Half sunk with all his Pines.
>
> 6.193–98

Milton must have admired Spenser's stanza a great deal, for in the Tenth Book he apparently alludes to it again, this time by imitating its rhetorical structure. We should not be surprised at the occasion — the metamorphosis of Satan's followers into serpents.

> . . . down thir arms,
> Down fell both Spear and Shield, down they as fast,
> And the dire hiss renew'd,
>
> 10.541–43

That Milton's exploitation of this material was systematic is confirmed by the fact that, throughout the entire poem, he never draws upon it except in oblique reference either to Satan or his followers.

We must now return to the description of Satan on the Burning Lake, where, "extended long and large," he

> Lay floating many a rood, in bulk as huge
> As whom the Fables name of monstrous size,
> *Titanian*, or *Earth-born*, that warr'd on *Jove*,
> *Briareos* or *Typhon*, whom the Den
> By ancient *Tarsus* held, or that Sea-beast
> *Leviathan*,
>
> 1.197–201

In the far background of this passage is Hesiod's account of the War between the Gods and the Giants. This war had been brought to a successful conclusion when the victorious Zeus hurled the Titans from the skies. For nine whole days and nights they fell from Heaven to Earth, and for another nine whole days and nights from Earth to Tartarus, the pagan version of Hell, where they had been doomed to eternal confinement. I have called attention elsewhere to the allegorical tradition which identified the Gigantomachia with the Revolt of the Angels.[18] There is even warrant for Thyer's view that Milton may have subscribed to the belief, widely held in his day, that the Gigantomachia owed its literary origin to "some uncertain clouded tradition" among the pagans of the War in Heaven.[19] Be that as it

---

[18] *Milton and the Renaissance Ovid* (Urbana, Ill., 1946), pp. 85–87.

[19] Cf. the note of Merritt Y. Hughes to *P.L.* 1.197, which I quote in part: "Both Titans and Giants were earth-born and were confused in the later accounts of the attack upon the Olympian gods. Milton's interest in the myth as well as his contempt for it may have sprung from his sympathy with the theory, by which Sir Walter Raleigh was influenced in his *History of the World* (I, vi, 8), that the gentile myths were perversions but also corroborations of the Mosaic records."

may, the powerful literary memories associated with the myth were too many and too vivid for Milton to leave them untapped.

> Nine times the Space that measures Day and Night
> To mortal men, he with his horrid crew
> Lay vanquisht, rowling in the fiery Gulfe
> Confounded though immortal:
>
> 1.50–53

The reference, of course, is to Satan and his defeated followers on the Burning Lake, whither they had been harried by the Christian God, armed with the thunder and red lightning of Zeus.

For the use which he makes of the Gigantomachia in the First Book, however, Milton's direct source is not Hesiod but, as so often has been the case, Virgil. In the Sixth Book of the *Aeneid*, Virgil tells of the descent of Aeneas into Hades, accompanied by the Sybil who serves as his guide. Eventually, the pair reach the adamantine gates of Tartarus. Through these gates — gates which, whenever they are opened, "grate on jarring hinge" (*horrisono stridentes cardine*)[20] — no pure foot may pass. The Sybil, therefore, from her own privileged experience, provides Aeneas with a graphic account of the horrors behind them.

Here Earth's ancient children, the Titans' brood, hurled down by the thunderbolt, lie wallowing in the abyss. Here likewise I saw the twin Aloids, enormous of frame, who essayed with violent hands to pluck down high heaven and thrust Jove from his upper realm. Likewise I saw Salmoneus paying the grim penalty for mocking Jove's flame and Olympus' thunders. Borne by four horses and brandishing a torch, he rode in triumph amid the Grecian people and through Elis town, and claimed for himself the worship of deity; madman! who would mimic the storm-cloud and the inimitable bolt with brass that rang under his trampling horse-hoofs. But the Lord omnipotent hurled his shaft through thickening clouds (no firebrand his, nor smoky glare of torches) and dashed him headlong in the fury of the whirlwind. Therewithal Tityos might be seen, fosterling of Earth the mother of all, whose body stretches over nine full acres, and a monstrous vulture with crooked beak eats away the imperishable liver and the entrails that breed in suffering . . . [6.580–98].

Although the influence of the passage is mainly felt in the lines which initiated this discussion, its ramifications are present elsewhere in the First Book of *Paradise Lost*. For example, it is hard to see how anyone could read its opening lines, even in translation, without associating them with the passage from *Paradise Lost* quoted in the preceding paragraph. Here the Latin is important.

---

[20] Cf. *P.L.* 2.879–82, where Milton tries to imitate the sound as well as the sense of this phrase in describing the manner in which the gates of Hell fly open when Sin unlocks them.

hic genus antiquum Terrae, Titania pubes,
fulmine deiecti fundo volvuntur in imo.

6.580–81

Except for the addition of the epithet, Milton's "rowling in the
fiery Gulfe" exactly translates Virgil's *fundo volvuntur in imo* ("lie
wallowing in the abyss"). Or again, the fate of Salmoneus as Virgil
describes it — Salmoneus who, because he aspired to godhead, was
smitten by a thunderbolt from the hand of the *pater omnipotens*,
Jove, and dashed headlong (*praecipitemque . . . adegit*) from the
heavens — recalls even in its very phrasing the fate of Satan:

> . . . Him the Almighty Power
> Hurld headlong flaming from th'Ethereal Skie

1.44–45

But we are mainly concerned with the repercussions of the Virgilian passage in the lines which describe Satan on the Burning Lake.
In this connection, it is surely no rash conjecture to suggest that
Milton's phrase *"Titanian, or Earth-born"* (1.198) probably had its
genesis in Virgil's *genus antiquum Terrae, Titania pubes*. For the
latter's "twin Aloids," Milton has substituted the names of two other
giants, Briareos and Typhon, whose histories were undoubtedly better known to his contemporaries. Both Briareos and Typhon had
made war upon the Olympians and, after their defeat, had been consigned to everlasting punishment, the one in Tartarus, the other
buried under Mount Etna. The allegorical history of Typhon, or of
Typhoeus as he was more usually called, is of particular interest.
Because he was the leader of the giants who warred on Jove, the same
tradition that identified the Gigantomachia with the Revolt of the
Angels identified Typhon with Satan and Mount Etna with Hell.[21]
This in itself would give Milton's comparison an added propriety,
but now a new element enters into the description. Both Briareos
and Typhon were monsters. Briareos is alleged to have had one hundred arms and fifty hands, and Typhon one hundred arms in addition to possessing serpentlike extremities. Obviously, Milton could
not have eliminated these damaging associations from his comparison. Indeed, it is plain that he did not wish to do so, for a moment
later he rounds off his sequence of comparisons with an allusion to
that "Sea-beast *Leviathan*." The word is derived from the Hebrew,
livyathan. As Milton, who knew Hebrew, must have been well aware,
the word in that language denoted any monster of the deep. But what
gathers the allusion significantly into the context of the passage is

---

[21] Harding, pp. 85–87.

a verse in Isaiah (27.1), where the Hebrew prophet predicts that the day shall surely come when the Lord "shall punish leviathan the piercing serpent, even leviathan that crooked serpent; and he shall slay the dragon that is in the sea."

The direct allusions in the passage, however, are not so important perhaps as the surreptitious ones. We have already discussed its connection with the Laocoon story. Hidden away between its lines is also an allusion to the legend of Tityos, whose prostrate body in Tartarus, according to Virgil, occupies "over nine full acres" (*per tota novem cui iugera corpus / porrigitur,* 6.596–97). Milton uses the same unit of land measurement (a rood, as Newton carefully points out, is the fourth part of an acre) in describing Satan's prone position on the Burning Lake, where, "extended long and large," he "Lay floating many a rood." On the face of it, the covert allusion to Tityos seems merely designed to provide another illustration of Satan's tremendous size. But I should guess that it would be improbable that the reader could visualize the size of Tityos without also thinking of his terrible punishment, particularly if Milton had succeeded in establishing the relevance of the Virgilian passage in the background. Such a reader, it seems to me, would be made instantly more alive to the intensity and hopelessness of Satan's suffering by having it translated, if only momentarily and by sly indirection, into the vivid terms of the mode of torture meted out to Tityos. For Satan has his vultures, too, as we are soon to learn, though they are not of flesh and blood.

I mentioned a little earlier the allegorical tradition which connected Hell with the interior of the volcanic mountain Etna. A few lines after the passage we have been discussing, Milton compared the acrid soil of Hell with the "singed bottom" of Mount Etna.

> And such appear'd in hue, as when the force
> Of subterranean wind transports a Hill
> Torn from *Pelorus,* or the shatter'd side
> Of thundring *Aetna,* whose combustible
> And fewel'd entrals thence conceiving Fire
> Sublim'd with Mineral fury, aid the Winds,
> And leave a singed bottom all involv'd
> With stench and smoak:
>
> 1.230–37

The *locus classicus* for a poetical description of Etna's volcanic action is a passage in the *Third Aeneid,* and editors often refer Milton's lines to this source.

> Portus ab accessu ventorum immotus et ingens
> ipse; sed horrificis iuxta tonat Aetna ruinis,

interdumque atram prorumpit ad aethera nubem
turbine fumantem piceo et candente favilla,
attollitque globos flammarum et sidera lambit,
interdum scopulos avulsaque viscera montis
erigit eructans, liquefactaque saxa sub auras
cum gemitu glomerat, fundoque exaestuat imo.

3.570–77

There lies a harbour, unstirred by the winds' entrance, and large; but nigh it Aetna thunders awfully in wrack, and ever and again hurls a black cloud into the sky, smoking with boiling pitch and white hot embers, and heaves balls of flame flickering up to the stars: ever and again vomits out on high crags from the torn entrails of the mountain, tosses up masses of molten rock with a groan, and boils forth from the depth below.

There is a general similarity between the two passages in the working out of the imagery of violence, and some similarity in detail; we may compare, for example, the use of the same metaphor by both poets to describe the interior of the mountain, Milton's "fewel'd entrals" and Virgil's "torn entrails" (avulsa . . . viscera). Still, the evidence for a direct borrowing is inconclusive. It becomes much less so, however, when we take into account the context of the Virgilian passage. And this context in turn supplies a new but related set of associations which continue the work of systematic disparagement.

In the *Third Aeneid*, Virgil tells how the Trojans, wearied by the ardors of the sea voyage, at length take shelter in a Sicilian harbor hard by Mount Etna. Sicily is the home of a race of one-eyed, cannibalistic giants called the Cyclops, who are godless, lawless, and pitiless. One of the most memorable episodes in the *Odyssey* deals with the adventures of Odysseus and his companions in the cave of Polyphemus, the wickedest of the Cyclops. It is to this story Virgil adverts, for with the coming of dawn, the Trojan mariners see emerging from the forest near the shore a wretched creature, dirty, worn with hunger, and meanly attired. This turns out to be Achemenides, one of the companions of Odysseus, who had been left behind when the others escaped from the island. He tells his tale of horror and, just as the last words have left his mouth, the Trojans see on the mountaintop

ipsum inter pecudes vasta se mole moventem
pastorem Polyphemum et litora nota petentem,
monstrum horrendum, informe, ingens, cui lumen ademptum.
trunca manum pinus regit et vestigia firmat:

3.656–59

shepherding his flocks a vast moving mass, Polyphemus himself seeking the shores he knew, a horror ominous, shapeless, huge, bereft of sight. A lopped pine guides his hand and steadies his footsteps.

Terrified, the Trojans hastily pull away from the island. Polyphemus, however, hears the swirl of the oar-driven waters and raises a loud outcry which brings the rest of the Cyclops in a menacing body to the shore. They are so huge "they fill the shore" (*litora complent*), and as his ship is moving out to sea, Aeneas vividly describes the impression they leave on him and his followers.

> cernimus astantis nequiquam lumine torvo
> Aetnaeos fratres caelo capita alta ferentis,
> concilium horrendum: quales cum vertice celso
> aëriae quercus aut coniferae cyparissi
> constiterunt, silva alta Iovis lucusve Dianae.
>
> 3.677–81

We descry the Aetnean brotherhood standing impotent with scowling eye, their stately heads up to heaven, a dreadful consistory; even as on a mountain summit stand oaks high in the air or coned cypresses, a high forest of Jove or covert of Diana.

These lines provide Milton with the substance for one of his noblest similes. As Satan "Darts his experienc't eye" through the serried ranks of angels drawn up, in response to his inspirational call for action, along the shore of the Burning Lake, he is moved to compassionate tears, pondering the great sacrifice they have made on his behalf and the sorry plight to which it has brought them.

> . . . yet faithfull how they stood,
> Thir Glory witherd. As when Heavens Fire
> Hath scath'd the Forrest Oaks, or Mountain Pines,
> With singed top thir stately growth though bare
> Stands on the blasted Heath.
>
> 1.611–15

This is Virgil's "dreadful consistory" — the Etnean brotherhood — adapted to the topography of Hell and the hopeless predicament of the Fallen Angels. One notices how appositely Milton has varied the terms of the figure. In the *Aeneid*, the Cyclops are likened to trees which are alive and flourishing, not blasted and dying as are the forest oaks and mountain pines to which Milton compares the Fallen Angels. Most readers will agree that the change has been for the better. It improves the visual image. A forest of fire-swept trees bears a greater resemblance to an army of defeated warriors than a green forest and stands out in much bolder relief. But, more than that, the simile is accurate, recalling the full horror of the flight through Chaos when, pursued by the thunder winged with red lightning, the rebellious angels were being driven to their doom. "So much the stronger prov'd / He with his Thunder." The Fallen Angels had been literally scathed by "Heavens Fire."

We may now turn to an earlier passage, one which describes Satan's spear and the use to which he is constrained to put it, there on the burning soil of Hell as he moves forward to address his followers.

> His Spear, to equal which the tallest Pine
> Hewn on *Norwegian* hills, to be the Mast
> Of some great Ammiral, were but a wand,
> He walkt with to support uneasie steps
> Over the burning Marle,
>
> 1.292–96

If this passage does not conjure up a mental picture of Polyphemus on the mountaintop, steadying his footsteps with a lopped pine (*trunca manum pinus regit et vestigia firmat*, 3.659), it has not communicated its full meaning to us. So Satan steadies his footsteps with his spear — a spear, moreover, so long that it dwarfs the tallest Norwegian *pine* hewn down to make the mast of some great "Ammiral."

This comparison we do not find in the *Aeneid*. We find it, instead, in the *Odyssey*. There the club of Polyphemus, made of green olive-wood, is also likened to the mast of a ship (p. 135). Milton has first amalgamated, then magnified, details from both poems. By borrowing at this point from Homer as well as Virgil, he is able to release a whole new flood of relevant associations. For only in the *Odyssey* do we actually see Polyphemus about his bloodthirsty deeds. In the *Aeneid* the story is briefly told and at second hand through the medium of Achemenides, and the full dramatic horror of the tale as Homer had recounted it is never quite realized.

The first reference to Satan in *Paradise Lost* is to "th'Infernal Serpent" (1.34). Between this reference and the third line of the Fourth Book, where Milton alludes to Satan as "the Dragon" — in other words just before the soliloquy on Mount Niphates — he never once directly and openly identifies Satan as the Serpent. But if it is the Lucifer-in-Satan which, in the beginning, is allowed to engage our attention, it is also true that Milton never lets us forget for long that the qualities of the Serpent coexist in Satan along with those of Lucifer, poised and ready, when the right time comes, to perform their work of fraud and destruction.

So splendid is the poetry which Milton puts in the mouth of the orators who take part in the Infernal Council (2.1–505) that it is a common experience for readers to be moved in spite of themselves. Even Milton feels constrained to give the devils their due.

> O shame to men! Devil with Devil damn'd
> Firm concord holds, men onely disagree
> Of Creatures rational, though under hope
> Of heavenly Grace: and God proclaiming peace,

Yet live in hatred, enmity, and strife
Among themselves, and levie cruel warres,
Wasting the Earth, each other to destroy:

2.496–502

But he had in mind the *Fifteenth Satire* of Juvenal and this passage:

Sed iam serpentum maior concordia, parcit
cognatis maculis similis fera; quando leoni
fortior eripuit vitam leo? quo nemore umquam
expiravit aper maioris dentibus apri?

lines 159–62

But in these days there is more amity among serpents than among men; wild beasts are merciful to beasts spotted like themselves. When did the stronger lion ever take the life of the weaker? In what wood did a boar ever breathe his last under the tusks of a boar bigger than himself? [22]

As usual, the covert allusion qualifies the surface statement; it is Milton's way of urging us to keep our values straight. This method of doing so is far more effective than the interpolated moral condemnation, the denigrating word or phrase or passage, as when in the present instance after Belial's great speech in the Council, Milton strives to counteract its effect by supplying his own interpretation:

Thus *Belial* with words cloath'd in reasons garb
Counsel'd ignoble ease, and peaceful sloath,
Not peace:

2.226–28

After the Council and the ratification of his decision to seek out Paradise alone, Satan flies upward to the roof of Hell. There at the gates he meets Sin and Death. The latter exchanges angry words with Satan and, for a moment, they are on the verge of battle. Death on one side grows ten times more deformed and

. . . on th'other side
Incenc't with indignation *Satan* stood
Unterrifi'd, and like a Comet burn'd,
That fires the length of *Ophiucus* huge
In th'Arctick Sky, and from his horrid hair
Shakes Pestilence and Warr.

2.706–11

The comparison of a warrior in his glittering armor to a comet was a favorite with classical poets and it is impossible for that reason to trace Milton's specific indebtedness. The closest parallel is again with a passage in the *Aeneid*. Turnus and his Ausonian captains watch anxiously as Aeneas comes sailing in to shore.

ardet apex capiti cristisque a vertice flamma
funditur et vastos umbo vomit aureus ignis:

---

[22] G. G. Ramsay's translation in the Loeb edition of *Juvenal and Persius*, 1928.

non secus ac liquida si quando nocte cometae
sanguinei lugubre rubent, aut Sirius ardor
ille sitim morbosque ferens mortalibus aegris
nascitur et laevo contristat lumine caelum.

10.270–75

His helmet-spike blazes, flame pours from the cresting plumes, and the golden shield-boss spouts floods of fire; even as when in transparent night comets glow blood-red and drear, or the spendour of Sirius, that brings drought and sicknesses on wretched men, rises and saddens the sky with malignant beams.

If, as seems probable, this is the source for Milton's simile, he has clearly followed his almost invariable practice of expanding its terms. It is the armor of Aeneas which blazes forth like a comet but, in the passage from *Paradise Lost*, Satan is compared to the comet itself. Partly because of this, partly because of the way Milton has organized his lines, there is a great gain in vividness and in the sense we derive of Satan's awesome violence and terrible destructive energies. Nor should we fail to note how aptly the comet simile illustrates the celestial brightness of Satan and his great size. But why does Milton represent the comet as firing the length of the constellation Ophiucus "In th'Arctick Sky"? Why Ophiucus in particular? And why does he place the constellation in the northern sky when, in fact, it is not there at all, as Milton surely knew? These are not, however, mere ornamental details; they are Milton's attempt to convey additional overtones of meaning into his simile. Ophiucus, which metaphorically encloses the blazing Satan, is the Greek word for "serpent bearer." And Milton was willing to risk the astronomical error of assigning Ophiucus to a place in the Arctic sky because, according to the tradition which he makes use of elsewhere in the poem (see 5.689), Satan was the ruler of the north parts of Heaven.

After Satan has successfully negotiated the region of Chaos, he momentarily pauses on the outer shell of the created universe and gazes down in awe and admiration at the wonders stretched out below "from pole to pole." Then

> . . . without longer pause
> Down right into the Worlds first Region throws
> His flight precipitant, and windes with ease
> Through the pure marble Air his oblique way
> Amongst innumerable Starrs,

3.561–65

The scene vividly recalls a fine descriptive passage in the First Book of the *Georgics*. There Virgil describes the universe as it would look to an observer on the sun. He makes reference to its twin poles.

Hic vertex nobis semper sublimis; at illum
sub pedibus Styx atra videt Manesque profundi.
Maximus hic flexu sinuouso elabitur Anguis
circum perque duas in morem fluminis Arctos,

1.242–45

This pole of ours is ever uplifted; but the other black Styx and the deep
world of ghosts see underneath their feet. Here the enormous Serpent
glides forth, wreathing his coils in fashion of a river around and beneath
the two Bears. . . .

A few lines later Virgil mentions the "marble sea" (*marmor*). Newton compares this use of the word with Milton's expression "pure
marble Air" and also cites Virgil's *Hic vertex nobis semper sublimis*
(1.242) in connection with Milton's inability (3.574–76) to say
whether Satan went "up or downe / By center, or eccentric" in passing through the firmament. The reader who visualizes the universal
scene as Virgil depicts it would be certain, I believe, to associate the
enormous Serpent winding its coils around and between the two
Bears with Milton's description of Satan winding "his oblique way /
Amongst innumerable Starrs."

By such means does Milton suggest the presence of those monstrous qualities in Satan which are not permitted to come directly
and fully to the surface until he bares his soul in the privacy of Mount
Niphates and his awful secret is out at last. A word should be said
about this famous soliloquy itself. It has been pointed out that it
bears a certain resemblance to Homer's evocation of Hector's
troubled thoughts as he awaits the coming of Achilles. Recklessness,
bred of despair, is the prevailing mood of both Hector and Satan.
Each contemplates submission and each rejects it for the same reason:
their fear of that disgrace in the eyes of their followers which, in the
heroic code, is far worse than death or defeat. Hector then thinks of
the possibility of a negotiated peace with Achilles as Satan debates
the possibility of reconcilement with God. Both in the end decide
to pursue a positive course of action — positive without hope.

The reader who connected the two soliloquies in his mind would
perhaps also recall the simile which prefaces the description of Hector's mood and indeed helps to interpret it.

As a serpent of the mountains upon his den awaiteth a man, having fed on
evil poisons, and fell wrath hath entered into him, and terribly he glareth
as he coileth himself about his den, so Hector with courage unquenchable
gave not back, leaning his shining shield against a jutting tower [*Iliad*,
p. 403].

CHAPTER FOUR

The Veil of Innocence

Before complying with Adam's request for an account of the Creation, Raphael warns him that he must not interpret what he says too literally, for

> . . . to recount Almightie works
> What words or tongue of Seraph can suffice,
> Or heart of man suffice to comprehend?
>
> 7.112–14

If so articulate an angel as Milton's Raphael could not make comprehensible to Adam, intellectually and morally "the goodliest man of men since born," the high mystery of the Creation, it is not likely that the poet himself was under the impression that he could provide a logical explanation for the mystery of the Fall to Fallen Humanity. When we are tempted, therefore, to feel that Milton on occasion has taken too much upon himself, we should in fairness submit our feelings in the case to the test of Raphael's words to Adam. Milton did not claim any special insight into divine truths. He knew well enough that, even had he been gifted with the "tongue of Seraph," it was not within his powers to make the Fall logically comprehensible. It was, however, within his powers to transcend man's finite understanding through the magical agency of poetry and to make the facts of the Fall imaginatively true and hence wholly acceptable, wholly believable, to those who would read the poem as a poem and not as an exercise in theology.

Milton, of course, believed in the historical truth of the Fall. He did not doubt that there was once an Adam, that God out of His great goodness created him in His own image, and placed him in the Garden of Eden to dress it and to keep it, that in the midst of the Garden grew the Tree of Knowledge of Good and Evil whose fruit God expressly enjoined Adam not to eat, that He fashioned a helpmeet for Adam out of one of his ribs, that the woman, tempted by the subtle serpent, transgressed God's sole command and persuaded Adam to follow her example, that by this act of disobedience, sin and death were born into the world, and finally that God in His just

anger expelled the sinful man and woman from the Garden. Milton
did not doubt that these events had actually taken place because
they were recorded in the first four chapters of Genesis. Here, then,
is the bare outline of the story which Milton proposed to commemo-
rate in epic poetry. It was clearly not enough. Milton had two main
problems: first, he had to provide substance for his skeletonic story,
and this substance he could either draw from his own mind or from
Christian and rabbinical commentary on the Fall, including the
hexameral literature, or from any source whatsoever, provided that
his imaginative reconstruction of events leading to and away from
the Fall did not distort or impair in any way the biblical account;
second, as an artist he had to motivate the Fall. He had to provide
a psychological bridge between a state of entire innocence and a state
of sin, between the Adam and Eve of the Fourth Book and the Adam
and Eve who awake one morning to find

> . . . thir Eyes how op'nd, and thir minds
> How dark'nd; innocence, that as a veile
> Had shadow'd them from knowing ill, was gon,
> Just confidence, and native righteousness
> And honour from about them, naked left
> To guiltie shame:
>
> 9.1053–58

Let me be more specific. The crisis of *Paradise Lost* is initiated
when Eve, yielding to the blandishments of the Serpent, plucks the
Forbidden Fruit and eats it. Earlier in the same book in which the
Fall occurs, Milton is at pains to stress the whole innocence of Eve:

> Daughter of God and Man, immortal *Eve*,
> For such thou art, from sin and blame entire:
>
> 9.291–92

Not many verses before Eve eats the Fruit, and after the Serpent's
initial assault upon her vanity, we are again reminded by Milton
that she is "yet sinless" (9.659), a phrase which assumes an added
significance from the fact that it had been earlier applied to Adam
(7.61), and for a like purpose: to clarify his moral status at a critical
moment. How can evil enter and take possession of minds in a state
of Original Innocence? Yet, if Milton has done his work well, we are
to feel horror at the Fall but not incredulity. It is the principal purpose of this chapter to show that Milton had done his work well and,
if there is a failure at this focal point in the poem, the failure is the
reader's and not the poet's.

Until Eve eats the Fruit, the poet and the theologian have been
working at cross purposes. As a theologian, Milton was compelled

to maintain a spotless innocence in Adam and Eve until that precise moment when Eve actually eats the Fruit. As a poet, he was compelled to anticipate the Fall by implying in both our first parents not only a predisposition to sin but the specific frailty out of which the sin could grow and take its shape, as a plant is formed from its seed. These two aims are clearly incompatible. Milton could not gain the one without losing the other, and by achieving either too explicitly he would lose the poem. The center would not hold. So Milton was obliged to work for some kind of compromise. To accomplish by artifice what could not be accomplished in fact, Milton sought to implant in the minds of his readers a secret, furtive, tentative uneasiness about Adam and Eve — not so much doubts as the shadows of doubts — while simultaneously maintaining the illusion of their entire sinlessness.

Adam and Eve, as we first see them framed against the background of the miraculous Garden, are as perfect as words can make them. Appropriately their moral perfection is reflected in a transcendent physical beauty.

> His fair large Front and Eye sublime declar'd
> Absolute rule; and Hyacinthin Locks
> Round from his parted forelock manly hung
> Clustring, but not beneath his shoulders broad:
> Shee as a vail down to the slender waste
> Her unadorned golden tresses wore
> Disheveld, but in wanton ringlets wav'd
> As the Vine curles her tendrils, which impli'd
> Subjection, but requir'd with gentle sway,
> And by her yielded, by him best receivd,
> Yielded with coy submission, modest pride,
> And sweet reluctant amorous delay.

4.300–311

These lines, which stun us with a beauty as compelling and unadorned as that of Eve herself, merit an extended consideration.

We notice at once that Milton, like Homer, has secured his effects without particularizing. The few details he has given us have been scrupulously chosen for their power to give the widest possible play to the reader's creative imagination. One notices, in addition, that each descriptive detail is subordinated to the one large, informing idea — the dominant position of the man in the relationship between Adam and Eve, a concept of central importance to the meaning of the poem. The passage, in other words, reflects Milton's strong classicizing tendency, that artistic compulsion which, in the definition of a recent critic, is "to surrender what is of the least moment to idea — the discrete, the adventitious, the exceptional — whatever refuses to focus, to converge, to articulate — in short, multiplicity and divarification." For the full satisfaction of this impulse, Milton could not have selected a more congenial subject than the Fall story. To have described Adam and Eve more minutely would have been to falsify his poem in two ways. First, it would have muddled its design. Adam and Eve, the human actors in the drama of the Fall, must be seen in a fitting relation to the background of infinite time and space and to the mighty forces marshaled for and against them. They must keep their place in the poem. Second, as Mr. Eliot has recently emphasized, Milton was simply not entitled to present Adam and Eve as ordinary human beings.

These are not a man and woman such as any we know: if they were, they would not be Adam and Eve. They are the original *Man* and *Woman*, not types but prototypes: if they were not set apart from ordinary humanity they would not be Adam and Eve. They have the general characteristics of men and women, such that we can recognize, in the temptation and the fall, the first motions of the faults and virtues, the abjection and the nobility, of all their descendants. They have ordinary humanity to the right degree, and yet are not, and should not be, ordinary mortals. Were they more particularized, they would be false. . . . [1]

It is unlikely that the contemporary reader could have read Milton's first description of Adam without associating it in his mind with Virgil's first description of Aeneas.

> restitit Aeneas claraque in luce refulsit
> os umerosque deo similis; namque ipsa decoram
> caesariem nato genetrix lumenque iuventae
> purpureum et laetos oculis adflarat honores:
> quale manus addunt ebori decus, aut ubi flavo
> argentum Pariusve lapis circumdatur auro.
>
> 1.588–93

Aeneas stood discovered in sheen of brilliant light, like a god in face and shoulders; for his mother's self had shed on her son the grace of clustered locks, the radiant light of youth, and the lustre of joyous eyes; as when ivory takes beauty under the artist's hand, or when silver or Parian stone is inlaid in gold.

Both poets emphasize the same physical details — the eyes, the hair, and the shoulders; moreover, Milton's description of Adam's clustering locks almost exactly reproduces the effect of Virgil's *decoram / caesariem*. But let us admit at once that this is slender evidence upon which to base a claim for a direct borrowing. We do better when we turn to Virgil's own source. As Renaissance editors

---

[1] *Milton Criticism*, pp. 321–22.

almost invariably pointed out in annotated texts of the *Aeneid*, Virgil is in this place beholden to Homer's description of Odysseus, whose "deep, curling locks" flow "like the hyacinth flower,"

And as when some skilful man overlays gold upon silver — one that Hephaestus and Pallas Athene have taught all manner of craft, and full of grace is his handiwork — even so did Athene shed grace about his head and shoulders [*Odyssey*, p. 93].

Here, by a general agreement of Milton's editors, is the source for Adam's hyacinthine locks. Here, too, is the source for the simile with which Virgil concludes his description of Aeneas. Milton could not, with dignity, make any use of the simile without degrading in some manner the Supreme Artist who created his hero. God is incomparable. But, in other respects, he seems to have assimilated and transmuted the substance of earlier descriptions. The imitation comes at an important moment in the poem, our introduction to Adam, and its purpose is unmistakable. Milton is renewing his challenge to the reader to test Adam and what he stands for against the acknowledged exemplars of human excellence, Aeneas and Odysseus.

The allusion is fully absorbed into its new context. Eustathius, with whose commentary on Homeric epic Milton was familiar, says that hyacinthine locks are black locks and, as Newton adds, this interpretation is supported by Milton's apparent wish to contrast, as sharply as possible, the physical appearance of Adam and Eve.[2] It is also true that Milton is concerned at this point to present Adam and Eve in the best possible light; and "hyacinthine," in its ordinary as well as its epic associations, idealizes the color of Adam's hair, just as "golden" idealizes the color of Eve's.

Like Milton, both Homer and Virgil characteristically avoid particularization in their descriptions of physical beauty; they prefer to suggest its presence obliquely, either by a comparison with some ideal form of beauty, human or superhuman, natural or supernatural, or by describing the reaction that beauty excites in a beholder, or by the symbolic beauty of clothes. It is interesting that Milton, cheated by the hard facts of Genesis of any opportunity to exploit clothes symbolism in Adam and Eve, makes up for the deficiency by ascribing symbolic or quasi-symbolic values to their hair. The fact that Adam's locks do not fall "beneath his shoulders broad" signifies his manliness. Eve's hair, descending in ringlets to her waist "As the Vine curles her tendrils," symbolizes her subjection to her husband. Milton, of course, was simply following St. Paul, who had said that

---

[2] See Newton's note to *P.L.* 4.301.

for a man to have long hair is "a shame unto him," but that "if a woman have long hair, it is a glory to her: for her hair is given her for a covering or veil." [3]

Upon this scriptural foundation Milton rests his first account of Eve.

> Shee as a vail down to the slender waste
> Her unadorned golden tresses wore
> Disheveld, but in wanton ringlets wav'd
> As the Vine curles her tendrils, which impli'd
> Subjection, but requir'd with gentle sway,
> And by her yielded, by him best receivd,
> Yielded with coy submission, modest pride,
> And sweet reluctant amorous delay.
>
> 4.304–11

The word "Disheveld," as used here, carries no suggestion of disorder or untidiness but simply means that Eve's hair is unconfined and hanging loosely (cf. "loose tresses," 4.497). The general impression we get is of an artless simplicity. But why "wanton ringlets"? Or, for that matter, the curled tendrils, which imply subjection, it is true, but also the kind of encroachment which may ensnare and destroy as well. I suggest, somewhat tentatively, that Milton, in this strangely troubling description of Eve, was seeking the richly ambiguous effect of Horace's untranslatable phrase, *simplex munditiis*, in the famous *Fifth Ode* to Pyrrha. "Unadorned, adorned the most," the yellow-haired Pyrrha combines voluptuousness with a sophisticated simplicity to conquer and betray the hearts of men. And Horace pities, at the same time that he envies, the unfortunate youth,

> qui nunc te fruitur credulus aurea
> qui semper vacuam, semper amabilem
> sperat, nescius aurae
> fallacis!
>
> lines 9–12

who now enjoys thee, fondly thinking thee all golden, who hopes that thou wilt ever be free of passion for another, ever lovely, — ignorant he of the treacherous breeze.[4]

We know that Milton was sufficiently interested in this ode to translate it.[5] The allusion, if there is one, merely deepens the impression, already implicit in the words and phrases used to describe Eve, of a lurking, potentially destructive sensuality. She may not be so artless

---

[3] I Corinthians 11.14–15.

[4] C. E. Bennett's translation in the Loeb edition of the *Odes and Epodes*, 1924.

[5] For an extended discussion of this ode, and Milton's translation of it, see below, pp. 128–31.

as she seems. But immediately Milton makes us almost ashamed of any suspicions we may have momentarily entertained.

> Then was not guiltie shame, dishonest shame
> Of natures works, honor dishonorable,
> Sin-bred, how have ye troubl'd all mankind
> With shews instead, meer shews of seeming pure,
> And banisht from mans life his happiest life,
> Simplicitie and spotless innocence.
> So passed they naked on,
>
> 4.313–19

"Then was not guiltie shame." These lines in the Fourth Book clearly look forward to the passage from the Ninth Book, quoted at the beginning of this chapter, describing the consequences of the Fall, when Adam and Eve, their veil of innocence stripped from them forever, are "naked left / To guiltie shame" (9.1057–58). To point up the parallel Milton has deliberately borrowed from himself, a technique which he probably learned from Virgil, who employs it constantly.[6] At the time when Adam and Eve first become aware of their sinfulness Milton momentarily transports the mind of the reader back to the wholly spotless Adam and Eve of the Fourth Book to strengthen the illusion that the transition from a state of innocence to a state of sin took place instantaneously, thus bypassing the intervening portion of the poem in which, with admirable tact, he has carefully prepared his reader for the exploitation of their fatal weaknesses.

This preparation, in the case of Eve, begins with the account of her birth. Eve tells Adam how she arrived at consciousness, full-grown, "Under a shade on flow'rs," not far from a gleaming pool. Looking into it she saw her own reflection in the smooth water and fell in love with it. "There," Eve continues,

> . . . I had fixt
> Mine eyes till now, and pin'd with vain desire,
> Had not a voice thus warnd me, What thou seest,
> What there thou seest fair Creature is thy self,
> With thee it came and goes: but follow me,
> And I will bring thee where no shadow staies
> Thy coming, and thy soft imbraces, hee
> Whose image thou art, him thou shalt enjoy
> Inseparablie thine, to him shalt beare
> Multitudes like thy self, and thence be call'd
> Mother of human Race: what could I doe,

---

[6] On self-repetition as a decisive factor in Virgil's style, see W. F. Jackson Knight, *Roman Vergil* (London, 1944), Chapter V, *passim*, but especially pp. 269 ff.

But follow strait, invisibly thus led?
Till I espi'd thee, fair indeed and tall,
Under a Platan, yet methought less faire,
Less winning soft, less amiablie milde,
Then that smooth watry image; back I turnd
Thou following cryd'st aloud, Return faire *Eve*,
Whom fli'st thou? whom thou fli'st, of him thou art,
His flesh, his bone; to give thee being I lent
Out of my side to thee, neerest my heart
Substantial Life, to have thee by my side
Henceforth an individual solace dear;
Part of my Soul I seek thee, and thee claim
My other half: with that thy gentle hand
Seisd mine, I yielded, and from that time see
How beauty is excelld by manly grace
And wisdom, which alone is truly fair.

4.465–91

The passage is based upon the myth of Narcissus as it is told by Ovid in his *Metamorphoses* (3.402–510). Narcissus is the youth who becomes enamored of his own image in a forest pool and, refusing to take his eyes off it, wastes away and dies. The moral is obvious, and in Milton's day as well as our own, Narcissus had become an arch-symbol for destructive self-love. As he so often does, Milton has accredited the borrowing by means of clear verbal echoes; he wants to be especially certain in this case that his readers will recognize the allusion and perceive its significance. At the same time he could not venture an out-and-out comparison with Narcissus, for that might well produce an impression of sinful vanity whereas Milton sought merely to establish a velleity. Eve is saved, as Narcissus is not, by a warning voice, and it would be a captious reader indeed who, recalling Eve's "unexperienc't thought," would be inclined to read too much into this trifling display of natural vanity. Milton himself invites the reader — virtually compels him, in fact — to underplay the vanity motif by permitting it to become swallowed up and almost lost in the professed moral of the episode, which is to impress upon Eve

How beauty is excelld by manly grace
And wisdom, which alone is truly fair

4.490–91

But a certain amount of damage has been done. We can no longer feel altogether easy in our minds about Eve.

Nor is our uncertainty likely to be allayed by the reflection that, to a surprising degree, Eve's birth is reminiscent of Sin's, described in the Second Book. In order to convict Satan of sole responsibility for the birth of Sin, Milton adapts the well-known legend of the birth of Pallas Athene, who was fabled to have sprung, fully armed, from the head of Zeus. "All on a sudden," Sin reminds Satan, when they meet at Hell gate,

> . . . miserable pain
> Surpris'd thee, dim thine eyes, and dizzie swumm
> In darkness, while thy head flames thick and fast
> Threw forth, till on the left side op'ning wide,
> Likest to thee in shape and count'nance bright,
> Then shining heav'nly fair, a Goddess arm'd
> Out of thy head I sprung: amazement seis'd
> All th' Host of Heav'n; back they recoild affraid
> At first, and call'd me *Sin*, and for a Sign
> Portentous held me; but familiar grown,
> I pleas'd, and with attractive graces won
> The most averse, thee chiefly, who full oft
> Thy self in me thy perfect image viewing
> Becam'st enamour'd,
>
> 2.752–65

As Satan is the sole "Author" of Sin (2.864), so Adam is Eve's sole author (4.635). Both Sin and Eve are, at their birth, full-grown and ravishingly beautiful, and both have been created in the image of their progenitors. But the most striking correspondence is that each is described as having been born from the *left* side. Now, on the theory that the rib from which Eve was fashioned must have been extracted from a region near Adam's heart, most commentators on Genesis had concluded that the rib was taken from the left side. Milton apparently subscribed to this view. But, so far as I have been able to discover, no mythographer had ever designated the side of the head from which Pallas Athene was born. Milton very likely, therefore, invented this detail. Why? Does it not spring from an attempt to compel the reader to identify, however vaguely or transiently, Eve and Sin, or at least the abstract idea of sin? I can see no other reason for this curious parallel.

Another correspondence between the two passages has a more obvious function. Satan sees in Sin his "perfect image" and falls in love with it. Eve falls in love with the image of herself she sees in the clear waters of the lake. The reader of *Paradise Lost*, knowing the lengths to which Satan's self-love, issuing first in pride, then in *hybris*, then in the act of disobedience, has carried him, is entitled to wonder whether Eve's innocent self-love, an offshoot of her inexperience, may not be susceptible to the same kind of development. Will history repeat itself?

No passage in *Paradise Lost* has its complete meaning in itself. It must be studied in its context, and I do not mean the immediate one alone, but that larger context which is the poem. Such a statement, of course, applies to all good poetry. But it is especially applicable to Milton's kind of poetry, a poetry which exploits, for all it is worth, the technique of cross reference. That is why critics who isolate Milton's verses in the process of discussing them run the risk of doing him a grave disservice. There is another danger. *Paradise Lost* itself is only a fragment in a still larger context, the literature of the past; and before we can feel that we have exhausted the meanings latent or dormant in a given passage, we should also study it in relation to that framework. I should like to illustrate these remarks by considering at some length the implications of the passage which occurs immediately after Eve has finished the account of her birth.

> So spake our general Mother, and with eyes
> Of conjugal attraction unreprov'd,
> And meek surrender half imbracing leand
> On our first Father, half her swelling Breast
> Naked met his under the flowing Gold
> Of her loose tresses hid: he in delight
> Both of her Beauty and submissive Charms
> Smil'd with superior Love, as *Jupiter*
> On *Juno* smiles, when he impregns the Clouds
> That shed *May* flowers.

4.492–501

Few readers will dissent from the verdict of Thyer. "There is the greatest warmth of affection, and yet the most exact delicacy and decorum. One would have thought that a scene of this nature could not with any consistency, have been introduced into a divine poem; and yet our author has so nicely and judiciously cover'd the soft description with the veil of modesty, that the purest and chastest mind can find no room for offence. The *meek surrender* and *half-embracement* are circumstances inimitable." [7] So they are. Perhaps no poet has ever more compellingly secured the effect of innocent sensuality. The passage, however, does not exist solely to evoke a powerful visual impression of marital felicity. It is a link between Milton's first definition of the relationship between Adam and Eve, "Hee for God only, she for God in him," and a most important passage in the Eighth Book, when Adam, almost rhapsodically, confesses to Raphael that he finds Eve's sexual attractiveness overpowering.

---

[7] Quoted by Todd, note to *P.L.* 4.492.

He recognizes that "in the prime end of Nature," she is "th'inferiour," yet, he says,

> . . . when I approach
> Her loveliness, so absolute she seems
> And in herself compleat, so well to know
> Her own, that what she wills to do or say,
> Seems wisest, vertuousest, discreetest, best;
> All higher knowledge in her presence falls
> Degraded,
>
> 8.546–52

We have come a long way from that "superior Love" by means of which Adam was wont to exercise a delicate control over Eve's "submissive charms," and the stage is set for Adam's fateful capitulation to Eve in the Temptation scene. The passage in the Fourth Book thus becomes the backdrop against which we can measure the full enormity of Adam's confession to Raphael.

There is still the classical allusion to consider. We observe, first of all, its appropriateness in the context, an appropriateness which emerges all the more clearly when we refer the allusion back to its source. It is based upon a passage in the *Second Georgic*, in which Virgil describes the coming of spring.

> Tum pater omnipotens fecundis imbribus Aether
> coniugis in gremium laetae descendit, et omnes
> magnus alit magno commixtus corpore fetus.
> Avia tum resonant avibus virgulta canoris,
> et Venerem certis repetunt armenta diebus;
> parturit almus ager, Zephyrique tepentibus auris
> laxant arva sinus; superat tener omnibus umor;
>
> 2.325–31

Then the lord omnipotent of Sky descends in fruitful showers into the lap of his laughing consort, and mingling with her mighty body nourishes all her fruits in might. Then pathless copses ring with warbling birds, and at the appointed days the herds renew their loves; the bountiful land breaks into birth, and the fields unbosom to wavering breezes of the West: everywhere delicate moisture overflows. . . .

Milton has compressed this myth into two and a half lines and, while retaining the fertility concept, has eliminated the gross physical details which would have been out of place in the new concept. The purpose of the allusion is clearly to stress the status of Adam and Eve as the Universal Parents, from whom all human life springs, and in so doing to secure the impression of a healthy, normal sensuality. The sexual life of Adam and Eve is as innocent and purposeful as that of the Garden in which they are placed.

Nevertheless, the allusion is a puzzling one. Why, for example,

this early in the poem does Milton risk a comparison with Jupiter
and Juno, whose marital relationship was scarcely ideal even by
Olympian standards? It does little good to say that Milton had a
naturalistic Jupiter and Juno in mind; no amount of explicitness
could wholly protect the passage from the surreptitious intrusion of
the less flattering associations which had grown up about their names.
Furthermore, we notice — though at the time the fact seems of no very
great importance — that Milton has varied the terms of Virgil's image.
For the cloud-and-flowers metaphor by means of which he has communicated the idea of fertility we look in vain in the *Georgic* passage. Not, in fact, until after the Fall is the whole meaning of the
passage released.

After the Fall, the perilous balance between innocence and sensuality is upset. All decorous restraint is gone, as Adam eagerly solicits
— there is no better word for it now — the sexual services of his wife.

> But come, so well refresh't, now let us play,
> As meet is, after such delicious Fare;
> For never did thy Beautie since the day
> I saw thee first and wedded thee, adorn'd
> With all perfections, so enflame my sense
> With ardor to enjoy thee, fairer now
> Than ever, bountie of this vertuous Tree.
>
> 9.1027–33

What was once a mysterious rite (cf. 4.736–75), to be celebrated at
nighttime after the day's pleasant work in the Garden, has degener-
ated into sheer self-indulgence and amorous "play," to be enjoyed
any time, anywhere. It is small wonder that Milton, at this point,
should underscore the new development by alluding, powerfully
and unequivocally, to the most immoral episode in the *Iliad* — the
celebrated love-encounter between Jupiter and Juno on Mount Ida.
For so Jupiter had solicited Juno and in almost the same words.

Hera, thither mayst thou go on a later day. But come let us twain take pleasure in the bed of love. For never once as thus did the love of goddess or
woman so mightily overflow and conquer the heart within my breast [*Iliad*,
p. 259].

The story of Juno's betrayal of Jupiter on Mount Ida is told at
length in the *Fourteenth Iliad*. The Greeks, whom Juno favored,
had been for some time unable to make any appreciable headway
against the Trojans, but now, to bolster the Greek cause, Neptune
(Poseidon) proposed to enter the war on their side. Aware that Jupiter would not tolerate such brazen intervention, Juno determined to
secure his ignorance of it until the damage had been done. First, she

anointed her body with perfumes and then clothed herself in an ambrosial robe, the gift of Minerva. Then,

with a veil over all the peerless goddess veiled herself, a fair new veil, bright as the sun . . . [*Iliad*, p. 255].

And, finally, having "adorned her body with all her array," she borrowed Venus' fragrant zone and went to seek out Jupiter on Mount Ida,

and the son of Kronos clasped his consort in his arms. And beneath them the divine earth sent forth fresh new grass, and dewy lotus, and crocus, and hyacinth, thick and soft, that raised them aloft from the ground. Therein they lay, and were clad on with a fair golden cloud, whence fell drops of glittering dew [*Iliad*, p. 260].

Sated, Jupiter falls into a heavy sleep. Now the Achaians, led by the god Neptune, attack the Trojans and quickly put them to flight. The slaughter is great and even the formidable Hector is gravely wounded by a huge rock. Finally, Jupiter awakes and, looking down upon the carnage and perceiving the desperate plight of the Trojans, realizes that he has been betrayed. His love for Juno turns to resentment and anger, and he bitterly reviles her for her perfidy, minimizing all the while his own weakness and folly.

By virtually translating part of Jupiter's speech and putting it in the mouth of Adam, Milton seeks to draw his reader's attention to the infamous episode on Mount Ida. He then enforces the parallel by means of another imitation. Like Jupiter, Adam quickly translates his lascivious praise of his wife's beauty into active lechery.

> Her hand he seis'd, and to a shadie bank,
> Thick overhead with verdant roof imbowr'd
> He led her nothing loath; Flours were the Couch
> Pansies, and Violets, and Asphodel,
> And Hyacinth, Earths freshest, softest lap.
> There they thir fill of love, and Loves disport
> Took largely, of thir mutual guilt the Seale,
> The solace of thir sin, till dewie sleep
> Oppress'd them, wearied with thir amorous play.
>
> 9.1037–45

It is scarcely necessary to comment upon the sequel — Adam's harsh, vindictive condemnation of his wife, upon whom, Jupiter-like, his first reaction is to place the whole blame.

This parallel led Pope to comment on the superior judgment Milton had displayed in making one of the "exceptionable" passages in the *Iliad* the vehicle for a "moral lesson." [8] The implied comparison

---

[8] Pope's comment is cited by Newton in a note to *P.L.* 9.1029.

is especially valuable for the light it throws on Adam's motives, not after but before the Fall. Again it was Pope who was the first, apparently, to see that Milton's use of the Mount Ida episode was not confined to that portion of the poem immediately following the Fall. He recognized an earlier allusion in the Fourth Book, occurring, oddly enough, in Milton's description of the idyllic bridal bower to which Adam and Eve had once repaired in all their Original Innocence.

> . . . each beauteous flour,
> *Iris* all hues, Roses, and Gessamin
> Rear'd high thir flourisht heads between, and wrought
> Mosaic; underfoot the Violet
> Crocus, and Hyacinth with rich inlay
> Broiderd the ground, more colour'd then with stone
> Of costliest Emblem:

4.697–703

And Pope remarks that, in this passage, Milton reproduces not only the words but the cadences of Homer's description of the flowers which spring up beneath Jupiter and Juno (*Iliad*, p. 260). [9] If this is true, and there seems no reason to doubt that it is not, then the Mount Ida episode is a link between the two passages, the one in the Fourth Book illustrating sexuality before the Fall, the other in the Ninth Book commenting upon it afterwards. Here the contrast is, of course, vitally important, but Milton could have secured it without the allusion. In fact, it is precisely the allusion which imperils the contrast. Moreover, it is unthinkable that the allusion to the episode in the Fourth Book was, in any sense, an unconscious adaptation. If Milton knew what he was doing in the Ninth Book, he must also have known what he was doing in the Fourth Book. It follows that the earlier passage must therefore be part of the elaborate and largely secret machinery to prepare our minds for the Fall, and especially for Adam's part in it, since his is the "superior Love," his the responsibility not "fondly [to be] overcome with Femal charm," as Jupiter was on Mount Ida.

Under these circumstances, it would be well to look more closely at the earliest allusion, the one which initiated this discussion. And now, in retrospect, we perceive that it is by no means so innocent as it appeared on a first reading. Milton has employed Virgil's figure of speech, but he has changed its terms, substituting for them a new set of terms — the moisture-dripping cloud and the spring flowers —

---

[9] See Newton's note to *P.L.* 4.700. Newton concurs with Pope's view, to which he calls attention.

derived from Homer's account of the amorous dalliance of Jupiter and Juno on Mount Ida. The clandestine discrediting of Adam and Eve, we are forced to conclude, begins almost with the first lines which described them to us.

Thus, we are actully "prepared" even for Eve's dream, which E. M. W. Tillyard calls the first stage in her psychological fall.[10] It will be recalled that Satan had overheard Eve as she related the circumstances of her birth to Adam; it should therefore come as no surprise that so wily a strategist should concentrate his attack on the weakest point in the enemy defenses, Eve's innocent vanity. His initial assault takes the form of an attempt to influence her subconscious thoughts and desires. It is while Eve is asleep that Ithuriel and Zephon discover him

> Squat like a Toad, close at the eare of *Eve*;
> Assaying by his Devilish art to reach
> The Organs of her Fancie, and with them forge
> Illusions as he list, Phantasms and Dreams,
> Or if, inspiring venom, he might taint
> Th'animal Spirits that from pure blood arise
> Like gentle breaths from Rivers pure, thence raise
> At least distemperd, discontented thoughts,
> Vaine hopes, vaine aimes, inordinate desires
> Blown up with high conceits, ingendring pride.
>
>   4.800–809

Later Eve awakes, and tells Adam what she has dreamed. Puzzled and fearful, "with startl'd eye," she tells how she has dreamed, not this time of Adam as was her wont,

> But of offence and trouble, which my mind
> Knew never till this irksom night;
>
>   5.34–35

Before he can succeed, Satan knows from his own experience that he must first turn Eve's thoughts away from Adam and inward upon herself. So it is significant that, in Eve's dream, she cannot find Adam and sets out in search of him. At length she comes to the interdicted Tree and sees beside it "One shap'd and wing'd like one of those from Heav'n," who, to validate his claim for the beneficent virtue of the Tree, eats of its Fruit. Seduced almost as much by the epithets he adorns her with as by the argument that the Fruit will confer divinity upon her, Eve yields and eats:

> . . . Forthwith up to the Clouds
> With him I flew, and underneath beheld

---

[10] *Studies in Milton* (London, 1951), p. 11.

> The Earth, outstretcht immense, a prospect wide
> And various: wondring at my flight and change
> To this high exaltation; suddenly
> My Guide was gon, and I, me thought, sunk down,
> And fell asleep;
>
> 5.86–92

"My Guide." This is one of those key phrases with the kind of history in the poem which saturates it with meaning. Adam is Eve's guide, as she herself has always acknowledged, and it is shocking to find him replaced, if only in a dream. Again, "exaltation," as Milton has used it in this passage, has primary reference to the actual height to which Eve in her dream imagines that she has soared. But one cannot readily forget the many times in the poem that the word, in all its related forms, has been applied to Satan to express the *hybris* which had led to his ruin. And finally, we notice that in her dream Eve, like Satan, falls, or seems to fall, *physically*. Once more the urgent question presses itself upon us: will history repeat itself?

For Eve's dream there is no precedent in the literature of the Fall. The device, however, was an epic convention; Homer frequently employed it and succeeding poets as usual imitated him. Dreams were put to a variety of literary purposes. They might serve to warn, to foreshadow, or to motivate, but as a rule a dream performed only one of these possible functions, rarely two, never, I believe, all three at once. It is not surprising, therefore, that there is no single direct model in classical literature for Milton's dream. Doubtless he followed his usual practice of developing and synthesizing hints taken from multiple sources.

One of these was probably the dream of Turnus in the *Seventh Aeneid* (lines 406 ff.). In this dream Allecto, the most terrible of the three Furies of Hell, appears to Turnus and, on orders from Juno, poisons his mind against the Trojans. Insensate, Turnus breaks the peace treaty between the two peoples, thus precipitating the war for Italy which was to culminate in his own death at the hands of Aeneas. Eve's dream, like that of Turnus, bears directly on the crisis of the poem, and a verbal parallel increases the likelihood that Milton had his dream in mind. Just before Allecto appears to Turnus, she visits Amata, wife to King Latinus, and culling a serpent from her black tresses, slips it into the queen's bosom.

> ille inter vestis et levia pectora lapsus
> volvitur attactu nullo, fallitque furentem
> vipeream inspirans animam.
>
> 7.349–51

Sliding between her raiment and smooth breasts, it coils without touch, and instils its viperous breath unseen.

With Jonathan Richardson,[11] I believe that Virgil's *vipeream inspirans animam* suggested Milton's phrase "inspiring venom" to describe the poisonous activity of Satan at the ear of the sleeping Eve. The allusion has a special interest in view of the serpent metaphor which Milton elsewhere in the poem has consistently exploited to manipulate our attitude toward Satan.

Another dream which may have influenced Milton is Medea's in the *Argonautica* of Apollonius Rhodius.[12] Medea dreams that Jason has come to Colchis to make her his wife and to take her away with him. The dream reflects her subconscious desires and longings, for, although she does not know it, she has fallen in love with Jason. In her dream she resolves to aid him, realizing that by so doing she will be severing all ties with family and homeland. This is the first hint we have in the *Argonautica* of her subsequent flight from Colchis with Jason. She awakes in fear.

Lastly, there is the dream of Dido in the *Fourth Aeneid*. Dido's dream, told by Virgil in that delicate vein of brevity and pathos for which he is celebrated, comes upon her when she knows that she is on the point of being abandoned by her lover.

> multaque praeterea vatum praedicta piorum
> terribili monitu horrificant. agit ipse furentem
> in somnis ferus Aeneas, semperque relinqui
> sola sibi, semper longam incomitata videtur
> ire viam et Tyrios deserta quaerere terra,
>
> 4.464–68

Therewithal many a warning of wizards of old terrifies her with appalling presage. In her sleep fierce Aeneas drives her wildly, and ever she seems being left by herself alone, ever going uncompanioned on a weary way, and seeking her Tyrians in a solitary land.

Mr. J. B. Stearns comments on this dream as follows: "No more striking method of depicting the helpless plight of the queen could have been devised. Dido's essentially tragic character is set in relief, and the poet foreshadows the finale of the sad episode by a device which forms at the same time an effective prelude to the ensuing *coup de theatre*." [13] The statement is almost equally applicable to Eve, and perhaps some trace of Dido's terrible sense of isolation carries over into Milton's description of Eve's waking to find herself

---

[11] See his note to *P.L.* 4.804, quoted by Todd.

[12] For Medea's dream, and her frightened reaction to it, see *Argon.* 3.616–44.

[13] *Studies of the Dream as a Technical Device in Latin Epic and Drama* (Lancaster, Pa., 1927), pp. 31–32.

alone. But it is a point I should not care to press. My main idea in presenting these dream analogues from classical literature is not to show Milton's specific indebtedness to them but to allow the reader to see for himself how Milton has revitalized an old convention and built it solidly and impressively into the structure of his poem.

The multiple resemblances in detail between the dream temptation and the actual Temptation are a matter of common knowledge. The question is: what does Milton gain by employing the dream? Part of the answer has perhaps been supplied or at least suggested by the preceding discussion. In preparing us psychologically for Eve's Fall, Milton has proceeded with the utmost caution; there must be no abrupt transitions. So first through the device of the covert allusion he seeks to make us uneasy in our minds about Eve, and then by means of the dream he provides us with the kind of insight into Eve's subconscious desires and aspirations which will increase our doubts — increase them without, however, quite justifying them. We cannot be certain that our interpretation is the correct one. Adam will do what he can to assuage Eve's fears:

> Evil into the mind of God or Man
> May come and go, so unapprov'd, and leave
> No spot or blame behind:

> 5.117–19

And this explanation seems to satisfy Eve, but the reader is left with just the right degree of skepticism. In addition to its usefulness in helping to motivate Eve's Fall, the dream also helps to define more narrowly the motive itself. Satan's appeal, throughout the dream, is to Eve's pride, the latent aspiration to godhead. Now, in fact, we do see history repeating itself, though the ominous little drama is enacted in the obscure world of dreams. When, four books later, the drama is re-enacted — this time in the world of actuality — the reader's horror is intensified by the irony that Eve shall fail to remember the dream and Adam's interpretation of it. Suspense is achieved as inexorably, step by step, we see Eve being led down the familiar path to her ruin, and ours.

> So saying, her rash hand in evil hour
> Forth reaching to the Fruit, she pluck'd, she eat:
> Earth felt the wound, and Nature from her seat
> Sighing through all her Works gave signs of woe,
> That all was lost.

> 9.780–84

So Nature had responded to the momentous sexual union of Dido and Aeneas in the Fourth Book of the *Aeneid*. Milton, as usual, has revivified the allusion; he has made it illustrate the general truth that all Nature was involved in the Original Sin. But this is not its main function. Every schoolboy would have known, most likely by heart, the famous lines in the *Aeneid*:

> . . . prima et Tellus et pronuba Iuno
> dant signum; fulsere ignes et conscius aether
> conubiis, summoque ulularunt vertice Nymphae.
>   4.166–68

Primeval Earth and Juno the bridesmaid give the sign; fires flash out high in the air, witnessing the union, and Nymphs cry aloud on the mountain-top.

And Virgil adds: *ille dies primus leti primusque malorum | causa fuit* ("That day opened the gate of death and the springs of ill"). The allusion reminds us that between Eve's sin and Dido's there are no adequate grounds for comparison. For Eve made it all possible. Dido and every erring man and woman are her responsibility.

CHAPTER FIVE

The Club of Hercules

In the preceding chapters I have tried to show how Milton, by the deft employment of allusion and analogy, sought to prepare us for the roles Satan and Eve were to play in the drama of the Fall. The strategy was scarcely new. As Mr. J. T. Sheppard has pointed out, it dates back at least as far as Homer. Thus, we are made to feel from the very beginning of the *Odyssey* that the intolerable insolence of the suitors will one day be terribly punished and that Telemachus, the son of Odysseus, will have a hand in the meting out of justice. The poem is hardly under way when Zeus, addressing his fellow Olympians in words made doubly ominous by their prophetic cast and dramatic context, reminds them of the fate which overtook Aegisthus, the slayer of Agamemnon. Zeus is complaining that men are wont to blame the gods for sorrows they frequently bring on themselves.

Even as of late Aegisthus, beyond that which was ordained, took to him the wedded wife of the son of Atreus [Agamemnon] and killed her lord on his return, and that with sheer doom before his eyes, since we had warned him by the embassy of Hermes the keen-sighted, the slayer of Argos, that he should neither kill the man, nor woo his wife. For the son of Atreus shall be avenged at the hand of Orestes, so soon as he shall come to man's estate and long for his own country. So spake Hermes . . . [*Odyssey*, p. 2].

The resemblance between the situations of Orestes and Telemachus, here adumbrated, is confirmed by numerous parallels in the Third and Fourth Books of the poem, leaving no doubt as to the artistic purpose the developed analogy was meant to serve.[1]

Compared with Virgil's delicate treatment of foreshadowing in the Dido episode, Homer's device seems relatively crude. Elaborate as the development of the Aegisthus-Orestes parallel may be, it re-

---

[1] The analogy was first pointed out by D. J. Snyder, *Homer's "Odyssey"* (St. Louis, Mo., 1895), p. 16. It receives a fuller discussion in J. T. Sheppard, "The Heroic *Sophrosyne* and the Form of Homer's Poetry," *JHS*, XL (1920), 59, and in George E. Duckworth, *Foreshadowing and Suspense in the Epics of Homer, Apollonius and Vergil* (Princeton, N.J., 1933), pp. 46–48. The latter cites the pertinent passages and comments on their supporting role.

mains detached from the stream of narrative and does little or nothing to illuminate character. Its sole function is to suggest to the reader what is likely to happen, not why it was bound to happen. In preparing his readers for the tragic capitulation of Dido to her passions, Virgil, on the other hand, builds his foreshadowing right into the narrative. It is a part of the story, and cannot be detached from it. Sychaeus is not an analogy; he was Dido's beloved husband.

The best proof of Virgil's subtle art is that we do not really appreciate the importance of Sychaeus except in retrospect. When we first see Dido, we see her, not primarily as a woman but as the Queen of Carthage — proud, imperious, aloof, efficient, every inch the ruler. By degrees we learn that it is not so much her independence that she cherishes as it is the memory of her husband. This husband, we had been informed much earlier in the poem (1.343–52), she had loved "with an ill-fated passion" (*magno miserae dilectus amore*). Twice more, within the space of the few lines Virgil allots to the relationship, mention is made of her passion for Sychaeus, a passion so intense that it amounts to a disease (1.351–52). Then he dies, treacherously murdered by her own brother, and Dido flees to the shores of Africa. Not until Aeneas arrived on the same shores was her heart to be shaken again; and some of the most moving passages in the *Aeneid* describe her heroic efforts to control its impulses. But we, the readers, recalling the terms in which her first love was described, realizing the kind of woman she is, know that those efforts will not suffice. Other foreshadowing devices, as we shall see in the sequel, associate her growing love for Aeneas with impending tragedy.

Milton does not make any direct use, and very little indirect use, of the Dido episode. Of the indirect uses, we have noticed one at the end of the previous chapter. Another occurs in the Ninth Book. Eve has just persuaded Adam against his better judgment to let her go out in the Garden alone.

> Thus saying, from her Husbands hand her hand
> Soft she withdrew, and like a Wood-Nymph light
> *Oread* or *Dryad*, or of *Delia's* Traine,
> Betook her to the Groves, but *Delia's* self
> In gate surpass'd, and Goddess-like deport,
> Though not as shee with Bow and Quiver armd,
> But with such Gardning Tools as Art yet rude,
> Guiltless of fire had formd, or Angels brought.
>
> 9.385–92

Eve makes a charming picture, confidently setting out alone, but the simile, if it has done all its work, should give the reader pause.

Milton is here deliberately imitating a famous "showpiece" simile in
the First Book of the *Aeneid*, in which Dido, at the height of her hap-
piness, is ironically compared with Diana, the goddess of chastity.

> qualis in Eurotae ripis aut per iuga Cynthi
> exercet Diana choros, quam mille secutae
> hinc atque hinc glomerantur Oreades; illa pharetram
> fert umero gradiensque deas supereminet omnes;
>
> 1.498–501

Even as on Eurotas' banks or along the Cynthian ridges Diana wheels the
dance, while behind her a thousand mountain nymphs crowd to left and
right; she carries quiver on shoulder, and as she moves overtops all her
goddesses. . . . [2]

The oblique allusion to Dido harms Eve, for it underscores her head-
strong desires, but even more it harms Adam. We are reminded that
it was only by resisting the impassioned arguments of Dido, rendered
the more compelling by the fact of his great love for her, that Aeneas
was able to fulfill his divinely appointed mission. But Adam, at the
moment of his crisis, weakly yields to Eve's iron blandishments.

A few lines later Milton anticipates the tragic consequences of
Adam's remissness.

> O much deceav'd, much failing, hapless *Eve*,
> Of thy presum'd return! event perverse!
>
> 9.404–5

Here the English poet invokes a foreshadowing device familiar, from
Virgil's skilled use of it in the *Aeneid*, to every contemporary reader.
As a convenient example, we may take the very first time the reader
knows for a certainty that Dido's love is destined to cause her death.
From the moment she sees Aeneas in the Carthaginian feasting
chamber, she has eyes for no one else.

> praecipue infelix, pesti devota futurae,
> expleri mentem nequit ardescitque tuendo
> Phoenissa. . . .
>
> 1.712–14

Above all the hapless Phoenician, victim to coming doom, cannot satiate her
soul, but . . . she gazes and takes fire.

Though a less subtle instrument, the *infelix* formula performs a
function very like that of the analogy, alerting the reader to the
nature of Dido's tragic flaw and to all the innuendoes and signs
which Virgil will provide in the future to suggest that her weakness
is steadily assuming the upper hand.

---

[2] Virgil's simile is in its turn an imitation of one of Homer's. In the *Odyssey*
(p. 89), Nausicaa is compared to Diana. The Delia of Milton's lines is, of course,
another name for Diana, derived from the fact that the goddess was born on Delos.

Milton, in the passage above, patently imitates the Virgilian formula, though it has become somewhat Miltonized in the process;
the hint of a moral judgment present in the lines illustrates aptly
enough a principal difference in temper between the two poets. Every
one of Milton's adjectives, we may notice, is made to count. "Hapless" translates Virgil's *infelix*. The others all have ostensible reference to the innocent motives which induced Eve to part from her
husband, but hint delicately at those other motives, related to them
but far from innocent, which weakened Eve's defenses against the
Temptation — unwariness, presumption, perversity. Once more, this
time after the Fall, Milton has recourse to Virgil's lines. When Adam,
returning from his congenial labors in the Garden, hears Eve tell
what she has done, he is stricken with horror. But at first he keeps
his thoughts to himself.

> O fairest of Creation, last and best
> Of all Gods works, Creature in whom excell'd
> Whatever can to sight or thought be formd,
> Holy, divine, good, amiable, or sweet!
> How art thou lost, how on a sudden lost,
> Defac'd, deflourd, and now to Death devote?
>
> 9.896–901

The last half-line translates the ominous phrase, *pesti devota futurae*,
which Virgil had applied to Dido, and we know that Dido was present in Milton's thoughts when he was developing the character of
Eve. There is, admittedly, on the surface little enough of Dido in
Eve — little enough, that is, that we can point to; but there is unquestionably a good deal to remind us of Dido and her creator in the
way in which Milton has presented Eve to us. We know Eve better, I
believe, partly because Milton knew Virgil so well.

The extreme difficulty of "proving" such a statement pinpoints
a problem which, sooner or later, every student of influences must
face, however reluctantly. "Different authors," writes Dr. Newton,
"may possibly hit upon the same thought without borrowing from
one another. An author, of great reading especially, may be ting'd
and color'd as it were by his reading; his writings may have something of the taste of the books which he has read without his knowing it, as the stream partakes of the qualities of the earth through
which it passes." [3] Where the work of an imitative poet is concerned,
the problem is obviously going to be more acute; and the better the
poet, the more acute the problem. That is why *Paradise Lost* is, in
this respect at least, undoubtedly the most frustrating poem in the

---

[3] Note to *P.L.* 9.513.

language. No other poem is so full of ghost influences, influences instinctively felt to be present but which resist to the bitter end the tags which scholars would dearly love to attach to them. The assimilative genius of the poet has intervened, and confronted with at best only faint and tantalizing echoes, the critic is reduced to conjecture or to an honorable silence. And as if this were not enough, there is a further complication. We have no right to assume that what today appears as a ghost influence was necessarily one at the time *Paradise Lost* was written.

What is one to say, for example, about these lines in the First Book, which depict so memorably the utter rout of Satan and his followers?

> . . . Him the Almighty Power
> Hurld headlong flaming from th'Ethereal Skie
> With hideous ruine and combustion down
> To bottomless perdition, there to dwell
> In Adamantine Chains and penal Fire,
> Who durst defie th'Omnipotent to Arms.
>
> 1.44–49

Earlier in the study (see above, p. 59) I associated this passage with the fate of that misty Virgilian prototype of Satan, the fanatical Salmoneus. Are we not also, at this point, to recall the story of Phaethon, another and better-known victim of Jove's unerring thunderbolt?

> At Phaethon rutilos flamma populante capillos
> volvitur in praeceps. longoque per aera tractu
> fertur; ut interdum de coelo stella sereno,
> etsi non cecidit, potuit cecidisse vidit.
>
> *Met.* 2.319–22

But Phaethon, fire ravaging his ruddy hair, is hurled headlong and falls with a long trail through the air; as sometimes a star from the clear heavens, although it does not fall, still seems to fall.[4]

Or is this one of those "influences" which are so vague and nebulous that they defeat any attempt to label them? Despite the verbal echo (Milton's "Hurld headlong" virtually translating Ovid's *volvitur in praeceps* and being accorded, in fact, an identical positional emphasis in the line), how many readers would deduce the parallel? Milton's editors, significantly, make nothing of it.

Nevertheless, I believe that the parallel would have occurred to Milton's seventeenth-century reader, who was not only abundantly familiar with the myth in Ovid's picturesque rendering of it but — more important for us — with the moral and theological allegories to which it had given rise. I have called attention elsewhere to the alle-

---

[4] Cf. *P.L.* 1.744–46, where Mulciber's fall through space is likened to that of a "falling Star."

gorical tradition which linked Phaethon with Lucifer and have suggested that Milton quietly exploited the tradition at several key
points in *Paradise Lost*.[5] In any case, how easy the seventeenth-
century reader would have found it to make the transition from
Satan to Phaethon may be inferred from this capsule interpretation
of the myth by George Sandys. "This fable to the life presents a rash
and ambitious Prince, inflamed with desire of glory and dominion:
who in that too powerful, attempts whatsoever is above his power;
and gives no limit to his ruining ambition."[6] Under these literary
circumstances, I cannot see how the contemporary reader could have
failed to make the association; he was ready for it in a sense that we
are not.

Milton systematically employed the device of the covert allusion
whenever his great principle of decorum militated against the use
of the open allusion. Except on such occasions, he did not attempt to
disguise his borrowings; on the contrary, he flaunted them, an honest
maneuver, quite in keeping with the most enlightened critical views
on the subject of imitation. By borrowing from Homer, Virgil, and
others, Milton was paying his poetic ancestors the highest tribute it
was within his power to pay. But it would be a mistake to minimize
the competitive factor in his manifest imitations. Milton would have
been out of step with his age if he had not considered himself in
active rivalry with Virgil and Homer, whom he would try to "over-
go," should the opportunity present itself, by a reworking of those
purple passages which had been most admired by readers and critics
over the centuries. The competitive factor was far from new in the
psychology of imitation; the Roman poetic convention of *retractatio*
or "rehandling" was mainly grounded upon it. Classical poets, that
is to say, were quite as much interested in perfecting what had already
been said as they were in saying something new. They were constantly, in the words of Mr. W. F. Jackson Knight, "pitting their
brains against each other to say the same thing more and more
exactly and beautifully."[7] There can be no doubt that Milton, like
other traditionalist poets of his own time, reflected this psychology.

Milton's open borrowings may be classified under three headings:
the direct quotation, the metaphor or simile, and the verbal echo.

---

[5] Harding, pp. 14–16, 88–93.

[6] *Ovid's Metamorphosis, Englished, Mythologiz'd and Represented in Figures*
(London, 1632), p. 66. The first five books of this translation were issued in 1621,
the complete text in 1626. Sandys' voluminous commentary was not added until
1632.

[7] *Roman Vergil*, p. 74.

Let us begin with the most transparent form of borrowing, the direct quotation.

Milton seems to have availed himself of this poetic privilege whenever he thought he could preserve in English a certain power or beauty inhering in the original. So, in the description of Pandemonium, he takes over bodily Seneca's noble phrase *ampla . . . spatia* (*Herc. Fur.* 3.673), giving it the kind of rhythmical setting in his adaptation which makes the phrase light up as if by magic. Action and syntax cooperate perfectly to create the visual image.

> . . . Th'ascending pile
> Stood fixt her stately highth, and strait the dores
> Op'ning thir brazen foulds discover wide
> Within, her ample spaces, o're the smooth
> And level pavement:
>
> 1.722–26

Or, again, when he translates Virgil's *lucentemque globus lunae* as "the moon's resplendent globe," it must have been the sheer verbal beauty of the phrase which fascinated him. But such instances are exceptional. Most of Milton's borrowings will be found, upon reflection, either to have absorbed a new meaning from their context in *Paradise Lost* or to have contributed a new meaning to that context. And this is as true of translated words and phrases as it is of the more subtle forms of borrowing.

Thus, Horace in one of his odes (1.2.3–4) describes Jupiter as having a "red right hand" (*rubente dextera*). When the phrase turns up in *Paradise Lost*, we find it where we might logically have expected to find it — in the mouth of one of the Fallen Angels, the infamous Belial, who is of course alluding to God.

> What if the breath that kindl'd those grim fires
> Awak'd should blow them into sevenfold rage
> And plunge us in the flames? or from above
> Should intermitted vengeance arm again
> His red right hand to plague us?
>
> 2.170–74

Here, obviously, the meaning of the phrase is not restricted to its mere descriptive function. It reflects the fear and hatred of the Fallen Angels and also their habitual tendency to discredit God by loading their references to him with just such vivid, emotive, highly charged words as "red" is in its context.

Again, when Beelzebub recalls to his own satisfaction the valorous deeds done by the insurgent angels in the Celestial War, he claims that they "endanger'd Heav'ns perpetual King" (1.131). The more usual epithet would have been "eternal," which, we might note, would also have fulfilled the metrical requirements of the line. Why, then, does Beelzebub substitute the word "perpetual"? Newton supplies the following convincing explanation. "The reader should remark here," he observes, "the propriety of the word *perpetual*. Beelzebub doth not say *eternal king*, for then he could not have boasted of *indangering* his kingdom: but he endevors to detract as much as he can from God's everlasting dominion, and calls him only *perpetual king*, king from time immemorial or without interruption, as Ovid says *perpetuum carmen* (*Met.* 1.4)."[8] For a similar reason, Satan in the first two books of *Paradise Lost* cannot bring himself to call God by his right name, which would imply more than Satan can bear to think of, just as the old man in Eliot's *Gerontion* attempts to evade the issue of death by inventing circumlocutions for the word itself. So when Satan confers Jupiter's title of the "Thunderer" upon God (e.g. 2.28), he is being evasive as well as derogatory.

> . . . so much the stronger prov'd
> He with his Thunder:
>
> 1.92–93

The thunder, of course, has not made God stronger but it is convenient for Satan to think so.

There are at least two other reasons why Milton resorts to translation. Sometimes he may do so in order to stamp a word with its Latin signification, thereby often adding a new dimension to its possible meanings. Thus, in the First Book of *Paradise Lost*, Milton refers to the "horrent Arms" of the Fallen Angels, presumably a rendering of some such phrase as Virgil's *Horrentia Martis arma* (*Aen.* 1.4; "the terrible arms of Mars").[9] By translating "horrent" Milton is able to keep the concrete meaning of the word intact: "prickly, set up like the bristles of a wild boar." This metaphorical sense of "horrent" may be conveniently illustrated by another quotation from the *Aeneid*. The Ausonian warrior, Asilas, *mille rapit densos acie atque horrentibus hastis* (10.178), which Mackail translates "draws a thousand men after him in serried ranks bristling with spears." We may note the obvious attempt on the part of the translator to preserve

---

[8] Note to *P.L.* 1.131.

[9] The lines in which this phrase occurs do not appear in manuscripts of the *Aeneid* before the ninth or tenth century. Mackail believes that they are Virgilian "in style and substance" but adds that we have no way of knowing whether Virgil had any intention of retaining them. Renaissance editors of the *Aeneid* discuss the problem of their authenticity at length. Milton would certainly have known the passage.

the metaphor. Only by translating *horrentia* as "horrent" could Milton have salvaged both the concrete and abstract meanings of the word.

At yet other times, he may use a word in an unfamiliar, or narrowly etymological, sense, as a kind of Ariadne's thread to lead us back to its source in one of the classical poets. This source will then often be found to have a substantial bearing upon the interpretation of the pertinent lines in *Paradise Lost*. For instance, at Hell gate Death bars Satan's way, demanding to know whether he is not that traitor angel who of late

> . . . in proud rebellious Arms
> Drew after him the third part of Heav'ns Sons
> Conjur'd against the highest,
>
> 2.691–93

"Conjur'd" here is too restricted by its local context to release more than its literal Latin meaning of "bound together by oath." Milton's contemporary readers would have needed no gloss to understand the meaning of the word, and not a few of them might have recognized its source. It derives from a passage in the *Georgics*. There Virgil is urging farmers to abstain from labor on the fifth day of every month; the fifth day is an unlucky one.

> . . . tum partu Terra nefando
> Coeumque Iapetumque creat saevumque Typhoea,
> et coniuratos caelum rescindere fratres.
>
> 1.278–80

On it earth bore that accursed brood, Coeus and Iapetus and fell Typhoeus, and the brothers that leagued [*coniuratos*] to pluck down heaven.

And we have another submerged allusion to the giants who warred on Jove. Nor is this the only sense in which the adaptation may be said to be typical of Milton. The main influence on the passage is biblical, "and behold a great red dragon. . . . And his tail drew the third part of the stars of heaven, and did cast them to the earth" (Rev. 12.3–4). These verses had always been interpreted by biblical scholars and commentators as an allusion to the revolt of Satan and his followers, and so too Milton plainly interprets them. In a passage which adroitly fuses the classical and Christian traditions of a War in Heaven, Milton has again sought to equate Satan with the Dragon.

Direct or, as they are sometimes called, open allusions are normally deflatory in character, whether they take the form of the drawnout epic simile or the highly compressed metaphor. Milton's similes have been closely analyzed. Mr. James Whaler has demonstrated, in a series of impressive articles, that unlike Homer's similes, Milton's are generally in contact with the subject they are illustrating at all important points.[10] They do not exist primarily to provide simple decorative or "background" effects, although they may work incidentally to that purpose. Rather, their main function is to interpret action or character, and often both, as in the following instance. When Adam wakes after taking his "fill of love" with Eve, it is to the knowledge of his terrible sin, and Milton is reminded of another wretched awakening.

> . . . so rose the *Danite* strong
> *Herculean Samson* from the Harlot-lap
> Of *Philistean Dalilah*, and wak'd
> Shorn of his strength,
>
> 9.1059–62

The simile precisely interprets the event and the motives which brought it to pass. Samson was betrayed by Dalilah but, as in the case of Adam, it was his own weakness, his overweening passion for his wife, which made betrayal possible in the first place. Hence, at the same time that it helps to clarify the motives for the Fall, the simile becomes the vehicle for a moral judgment.

Metaphorical allusions operate more economically, but often less strikingly, to the same general end. One of the most compressed of these allusions takes the form of a comment on the effect the Fall of Man had on the weather. Gone forever is that "perpetual Spring" which had been one of the beatitudes of Paradise.

> . . . At that tasted Fruit
> The Sun, as from *Thyestean* Banquet, turn'd
> His course intended; else how had the World
> Inhabited, though sinless, more than now,
> Avoided pinching cold and scorching heate?
>
> 10.687–91

The reference is to the most bloodcurdling of the old legends, commemorated in Seneca's play *Thyestes*, a most popular and influential work during the whole period of the Renaissance. At the feast prepared for him by his brother Atreus, Thyestes unwittingly eats the cooked flesh of his sons, slain by Atreus. Here, in concentrating a whole myth into one potent phrase, Milton invests Eve's act of eating the Fruit with all the horror and indignation evoked by the memory of that myth. But the more important function of the phrase is to

---

[10] See especially "The Miltonic Simile," *PMLA*, XLVI, No. 4 (December, 1931), 1034–74, *passim*. On p. 1065 Whaler says: "The key to fundamental difference between complex simile as found in Homer and in Milton lies in Milton's predominant method of exact homologation."

communicate, in retrospect, some of its horror to earlier lines describing Eve's gluttonous eating of the Fruit.

> Greedily she ingorg'd without restraint,
> And knew not eating Death:
>
> 9.791–92

A Thyestean banquet indeed, for Eve is metaphorically devouring her own progeny, the whole human race! *Paradise Lost* is full of such deliberate echoes.

But far more important than the direct allusion or quotation in Milton's scheme of borrowing is the verbal echo. The frequency with which these echoes occur in *Paradise Lost* has been fully documented by its editors; surely, on that subject at least, no more needs to be said. But one point warrants a special emphasis. No English poet, perhaps no poet except Virgil, has ever cultivated with more assiduity the art of verbal integration, the art of coercing two or more passages from one or more authors into a kind of fruitful collaboration with one another.

Let us begin with an example of integration in its simplest form. In order to intensify Adam's horrified reaction to Eve's admission that she had violated the divine edict, Milton skillfully weaves together two short passages from widely separated parts of the *Aeneid*. The one, coming at its very end, describes the dying Turnus, for all his faults the character in that poem who, next to Dido and Aeneas himself, makes the chief claim upon our sympathies.

> ast illi solvuntur frigore membra
> vitaque cum gemitu fugit indignata sub umbras.
>
> 12.951–52

But his limbs grow slack and chill, and the life with a moan flies indignant into the dark.

The other is from the beginning of the Second Book. The lying Greek Sinon, whose treachery was to lead directly to the Fall of Troy, tells the Trojans how the Greeks had reacted to the oracular utterance of Phoebus that the Greek cause could not prosper until the gods had been propitiated by the sacrifice of a human life.

> obtipuere animi gelidusque per ima cucurrit
> ossa tremor,
>
> 2.120–21

Their hearts stood still, and a cold shudder ran through their inmost sense.

By amalgamating phrases from each passage, Milton pools, as it were, all their relevant implications and brings them to bear upon the situation in his own poem.

> . . . *Adam*, soon as he heard
> The fatal Trespass don by *Eve*, amaz'd,
> Astonied stood and Blank, while horror chill
> Ran through his veins, and all his joynts relax'd;
>
> 9.888–91

The more normal procedure for Milton, however — and the one which was believed to provide the imitative poet with the best opportunities for displaying his skill — was to blend together materials from two or more different poets. Again let me illustrate. In the *Second Iliad*, Homer describes the effect which Agamemnon's words have on his army of Greek warriors, assembled for a council of war.

And even as when the west wind cometh to stir a deep cornfield with violent blast, and the ears bow down, so was all the assembly stirred [*Iliad*, p. 23].

Milton remembered this simile and rehandled it in the Fourth Book of *Paradise Lost* — though, as Brinsley would have put it, to a different purpose. Gabriel has just warned Satan that he would drag him back to Hell in chains unless he departed immediately from the precincts of Paradise.

> While thus he spake, th'Angelic Squadron bright
> Turnd fierie red, sharpning in mooned hornes
> Thir Phalanx, and began to hemm him round
> With ported Spears, as thick as when a field
> Of *Ceres* ripe for harvest waving bends
> Her bearded Grove of ears, which way the wind
> Swayes them;
>
> 4.977–83

Agamemnon's speech sways his audience irresistibly in one direction, as a violent west wind stirs a field of wheat. Since he is adapting Homer's simile to a new set of circumstances, Milton deliberately makes his wind a variable one to suggest the prevailing atmosphere of uncertainty. In Homer's simile, furthermore, the stirring of the warriors, and not their vast numbers, receives the major emphasis. Milton's simile, on the other hand, stresses both the stirring and the numbers, perhaps reflecting the influence of a passage in Virgil. Speaking of the Ausonian warriors assembled under the leadership of Turnus, Virgil records that they were

> vel cum sole novo densae torrentur aristae
> aut Hermi campo aut Lyciae flaventibus arvis.
>
> *Aen.* 7.720–21

as thick as the ears that ripen in the morning sunlight on the plain of the Hermus or the yellowing Lycian tilth.

Pretty clearly, Virgil himself was imitating the "cornfield" simile in Homer, and this makes it all the more likely that Milton had both similes in mind. But Milton improves on his models. Instead of applying the shafts of wheat to human beings, he applies them, more appropriately, at least from a visual standpoint, to the "ported Spears" of the angels. Even here, however, we may have to withhold full credit for originality from Milton. Virgil has much the same idea in one of his most striking metaphors.

> . . . Circum hos utrimque phalanges
> stant densae, strictisque seges mucronibus horret
> ferrea:
>
> 12.662–64

Round about them to right and left the armies stand locked and the iron field shivers with naked points.

To stamp his signature on a borrowing, Milton occasionally reproduces an ordering of words and phrases sanctioned by classical usage but artificial and somewhat strained when transposed into English. In the Fifth Book of *Paradise Lost*, for example, Satan awakens Beelzebub with these words:

> Sleepst thou Companion dear, what sleep can close
> Thy eye-lids? and remembrest what Decree
> Of yesterday, so late hath past the lips
> Of Heav'ns Almightie.
>
> 5.673–76

Then he urges his lieutenant to assemble the angels who have acknowledged him as their chief in preparation for the first show of force against God.

The lines are reminiscent of two passages. In the *Iliad* a Dream in the shape of Nestor informs Agamemnon that the differences between the gods have been settled and that the time is ripe for a decisive attack on the bastions of Troy. The Dream begins his address to Agamemnon on a similar note of petulant disapprobation. "Sleepest thou, son of wise Atreus tamer of horses?" (*Iliad*, p. 19). But Milton has given this verse a rhetorical cast which he derived from Virgil's imitation of it. As the Dream had approached Agamemnon, so Mercury accosted Aeneas in the course of a dream.

> nate dea, potes hoc sub casu ducere somnos,
> nec quae te circum stent deinde pericula cernis,
> demens. . . .
>
> 4.560–62

Goddess-born, canst thou sleep on in such danger? and seest not the coming perils that hem thee in, madman!

And again, Milton has both Homer and Virgil significantly working for him.

In the above passage, Mercury calls Aeneas a madman (*demens*) to bring home to him the folly of settling down in Carthage with Dido. On the surface, the word seems merely to reflect Mercury's irritation and impatience, but its literary history would have made it impossible for Virgil's contemporaries to give the expression a casual or unreflective interpretation. *Demens* is the Latin equivalent of one of the most important of Homer's formula words, *impios*, which the latter used whenever he wished to express his scorn of a character who, swayed by pride or self-confidence, was pursuing a course which could lead only to his destruction. Usually, Homer accompanies the word with a hint that the consequences of his action will be not at all what he expects.[11] Both Virgil and Milton follow Homer.

There is a particularly interesting case of Milton's use of the formula in the Sixth Book, which has the War in Heaven for its principal subject. He has just described Satan in the midst of his army of rebel angels.

> High in the midst exalted as a God
> Th'Apostat in his Sun-bright Chariot sate
> Idol of Majestie Divine, enclos'd
> With Flaming Cherubim, and golden Shields;
>
> 6.99–102

Aroused by this impious imitation of godhead, Abdiel angrily rebukes Satan in these words:

> . . . fool, not to think how vain
> Against th'Omnipotent to rise in Arms;
> Who out of smallest things could without end
> Have rais'd incessant Armies to defeat
> Thy folly; or with solitarie hand
> Reaching beyond all limit at one blow
> Unaided could have finisht thee, and whelmd
> Thy Legions under darkness;
>
> 6.135–42

Milton's "fool" translates Homer's *impios* and Virgil's *demens*. Furthermore, Abdiel's rebuke is directly modeled on Virgil's description of the insane Salmoneus, who, "borne by four horses,"

> ibat ovans, divumque sibi poscebat honorem,
> demens, qui nimbos et non imitabile fulmen
> aere et cornipedem pulsu simularet equorum.
>
> 6.589–91

---

[11] Duckworth, p. 8.

he rode in triumph . . . and claimed for himself the worship of deity; madman! who would mimic the storm-cloud and the inimitable bolt with brass that rang under his trampling horse-hoofs.

This was that same Salmoneus who, for his presumption, was smitten by Jove's thunderbolt and consigned forever to Tartarus.

The allusion to Salmoneus concealed in the speech which Milton gives to Abdiel is more damaging to Satan than the speech itself. Nothing could injure Satan more at this point, when his pride is at its zenith and as yet not called to account, than a comparison with the preposterous, doomed Salmoneus. It is as if, for the reader, Abdiel's dire prediction was fulfilled in the same instance that he made it.

Of all Milton's uses of the classical poets, not one reveals more sharply his close study of them than the frequent imitations of some of their finest metrical effects. Thus, when Milton describes the breaking of Satan's sword in the first stages of his single combat with Michael, he is repeating an incident which takes place at the outset of the duel between Aeneas and Turnus. In this combat, Turnus strikes the first blow. Raising his sword above his head, he brings it crashing down on Aeneas. But the latter is protected by armor divinely wrought for him by Vulcan, the armorer of the Olympian gods, and it proves more than a match for the sword, which breaks into fragments.

> . . . postquam arma dei ad Volcania ventum est,
> mortalis mucro glacies ceu futtilis ictu
> dissiluit; fulva resplendent fragmina harena.
>
> 12.739–41

When it met the divine Vulcanian armour, the mortal blade like brittle ice snapped in the stroke; the shards lie glittering upon the yellow sand.

This passage, too, is in itself an imitation. Virgil, as Newton shows, was thinking of Homer's account of how the sword of Menelaus was shattered against the helmet of Paris (*Iliad*, p. 55). "The line in the original," Newton adds, "is so contriv'd, that we do not only see the action, as Eustathius remarks, but almost fancy we hear the sound of the breaking sword in the sound of the words." Virgil, however, abandons strict onomatopoeia in favor of another auditory device. He allows the full rhetorical weight of the sentence to descend heavily on the verb *dissiluit* and then fractures his line sharply at that point, bringing metrical meaning and literal verbal meaning into full accord with one another. It is interesting that Pope imitates Virgil rather than Homer in his translation of the *Iliad*.

> The brittle steel, unfaithful to his hand,
> Broke short: the fragments glitter on the sand.

One cannot imagine a finer tribute to Virgil's imitative skill, coming as it does from so excellent a craftsman in his own right and one who knew only too well the rigors of any attempt to recall Homer to vigorous life in an alien tongue.

Milton, too, imitates Virgil rather than Homer. In his combat with Satan, Michael shares Aeneas' initial advantage over Turnus; his sword comes from "the Armoury of God" and was so tempered

> . . . that neither keen
> Nor solid might resist that edge: it met
> The sword of *Satan* with steep force to smite
> Descending, and in half cut sheere, nor staid,
> But with swift wheele reverse, deep entring shar'd
> All his right side;
>
> 6.322–27

The circumstances are slightly varied, accounting for the minor changes Milton has introduced. The swords of Menelaus and Turnus are shivered into pieces when they come into contact with the flat surface of armor. But, when Satan smites Michael, the latter intercepts the blow with his sword, the edge of which is so fine that it cuts the sword of Satan quite in half. Milton's principal imitation of Virgil consists in his attempt to convey the idea of shearing in half by a metrical maneuver; the pronounced break at the end of the fourth foot imitates the action of the sword. We may further note the circumstance that Milton has placed the half-line "and in half cut sheere" in such a position in the middle of the verse that it breaks it up into two equal parts, marked at either end by strong caesural pauses. The purpose is slightly different, but the poetical means are identical with those of Virgil.

It is necessary to emphasize that Milton is most characteristically himself when he uses such devices as we have been discussing not singly but collectively. To bring the total picture, therefore, into steadier focus, let us now consider a passage, one of a great many in *Paradise Lost*, which brings together into close collaboration all three principal forms of borrowing — quotation, direct allusion, verbal and rhythmical echo.

At a critical moment in the *Aeneid*, Jupiter commands Mercury to warn Aeneas that, by loitering in Carthage, he was defeating the will of the gods. Leaving at once, Mercury "courses the winds and swims through the tossing clouds" until at length he alights on the peak of Mount Atlas.

> hic primum paribus nitens Cyllenius alis
> constitit: hinc toto praeceps se corpore ad undas

misit, avi similis, quae circum litora, circum
piscosos scopulos humilis volat aequora iuxta.

4.252–55

Here the Cyllenian, poised evenly on his wings, first checked his flight; hence he shot himself sheer to the water. Like a bird that flies low, skirting the sea above the craggy shores of its fishery. . . .

At an equally crucial moment in *Paradise Lost*, God sends Raphael down to warn Adam of the enemy who is setting snares for him and to enjoin him once more to strict obedience of God's "sole command." Raphael immediately launches himself toward earth. "Down thither prone in flight / He speeds" (cf. these words and their ordering with Virgil's *hinc toto praeceps se corpore ad undas / misit*), and "with steddie wing" (cf. the expression *paribus . . . alis*) he rides the polar winds and "Winnows the buxom Air" (cf. Virgil's *ventosque secebat*, 4.257).[12] But Milton forgoes Virgil's simile of a sea bird skirting its fishery, which was scarcely dignified enough for Raphael. The bird to which he likens Raphael is none other than the *rara avis* itself, the one and only Phoenix.

> . . . till within soare
> Of Towring Eagles, to all the Fowles he seems
> A *Phoenix*, gaz'd by all, as that sole Bird
> When to enshrine his reliques in the Sun's
> Bright Temple, to *Egyptian Thebs* he flies.
> At once on th'Eastern cliff of Paradise
> He lights,

5.270–76

By placing the expression "He lights" in the first foot of the line, followed by a pause, Milton secures the same kind of rhetorical emphasis that Virgil had succeeded in imparting to his verb *constitit* (4.253) by an identical metrical device. In both passages, metrics has been brought to the aid of language to fortify the impression of a momentary physical pause.

A few lines later Milton relieves his readers of any fears they may have had that they were perhaps reading too much into chance parallels. Milton compares, outright, the graceful posture of Raphael on the eastern cliff of Paradise with that of Mercury, "Maia's son," on Mount Atlas.

> . . . Like *Maia's* son he stood,
> And shook his Plumes, that Heav'nly fragrance filld
> The circuit wide.

5.285–87

---

[12] See *P.L.* 5.266–70 for the whole passage from which these phrases are taken.

And finally, to seal off the parallel, Milton has Adam subsequently address Raphael as "Divine Interpreter." This phrase literally translates Virgil's *Interpres divum* (4.378), applied to Mercury.

Why is Milton so patently eager to have his readers recognize the parallel between Raphael and Mercury? There is, to be sure, the competitive factor; Milton must have wanted his readers to test the poetry describing the descent of Raphael against the corresponding verses in the *Aeneid*. But Milton is borrowing in this instance far more than mere words and phrases; he is, in fact, borrowing a whole structural principle.

In the *Aeneid* Mercury delivers his admonitory message, almost word-for-word as he had it from Jupiter, and departs as quickly as he came. Raphael, the "Sociable Spirit," however, proves more expansive than his literary prototype. In the process of communicating his message, he supplies Adam with a detailed account of the War in Heaven and of the Creation. This is Milton's way of catching the reader up on the events which antedate the plight of the Fallen Angels at the beginning of the poem. Thus, Raphael's role here exactly corresponds to Aeneas' when, at Queen Dido's request, he tells the story of the Fall of Troy and his subsequent wanderings up to the point of his arrival on the shores of Africa, in other words to the point where the action of the *Aeneid* begins. Raphael combines this function of Aeneas with that of the Divine Warner, Mercury.

By providing signposts so liberally, Milton makes certain that all his readers will recognize his indebtedness at this point to the epic tradition of Homer and Virgil and at the same time his entire willingness to be measured by its standards. The comparison, which Milton has been at such pains to drive home, adds up to a formal acknowledgment of that indebtedness.

Milton's borrowings, even the seemingly quite casual ones, cannot safely be ignored, for not only do they provide the critic with important insights into his poetic method, they also frequently serve to safeguard the critic from false or misleading interpretation. The famous bee simile in the First Book will illustrate the statement, I believe, on both counts. Milton compares the clustering of the winged angels about the gates, porches, and hall of Pandemonium to the swarming of bees about their hive. The Fallen Angels

> Thick swarm'd, both on the ground and in the air,
> Brusht with the hiss of rustling wings. As Bees
> In spring time, when the Sun with *Taurus* rides,
> Pour forth thir populous youth about the Hive
> In clusters; they among fresh dews and flowers

Flie to and fro, or on the smoothed Plank
The suburb of thir Straw-built Cittadel,
New rub'd with Baum, expatiate and confer
Thir State affairs. So thick the aerie crowd
Swarm'd and were straitn'd;

1.767–76

This passage has been criticized on the grounds of the impropriety of comparing angels, fallen though they are, with a swarm of bees.

Milton, of course, did not invent the bee simile. Its history in epic literature stretches all the way back to Homer, who compares the Achaian warriors, flocking forth in bands from the Greek encampment to hear what decisions their chieftains have reached in council, to bees issuing in tribes from a hollow rock.

Even as when the tribes of thronging bees issue from some hollow rock, ever in fresh procession, and fly clustering among the flowers of spring, and some on this hand and some on that fly thick; even so from ships and huts before the low beach marched forth their many tribes by companies to the place of assembly [*Iliad*, p. 21].

This passage probably gave Milton the idea for employing an imitative bee simile to describe the manner in which the Fallen Angels throng toward Pandemonium, *their* place of assembly. The general parallel is enforced in several particulars. Common to both similes are the clustering of the bees (Newton, in a note to *P.L.* 1.768, remarks that Milton's phrase, "In clusters," renders perfectly the force of the Greek *botrudon*), the flying to and fro, the spring flowers. It does very little good to say that Milton could have derived all these details from natural observation. So he could have. But, as we know, Milton did not habitually work in that fashion. We are dealing here again with an instance of *retractatio*. He wanted his readers to recognize the source of his allusion so that they could compare his version with the original and then judge for themselves how skillfully, and with what new creative insights, he had reworked it.

They would have seen at once that Milton's simile differs from Homer's in several ways. Milton's bees reproduce the movements of the Fallen Angels from the time they converge on Pandemonium to the moment when they are called to order. And the emphasis is not the same. The main point of the Homeric comparison is to express the numbers of the Greek warriors and the manner in which they come forward. It is exclusively a visual image. On the other hand, although Milton is making the same point, his simile engages the ear fully as much as it does the eye. We *hear* the rustling of innumerable wings and the busy humming, which is like the low murmur of statesmen sharing their views in an antechamber before some high conference gets under way. The effect is heightened by the onomatopoeia, produced by the massed sibilants, to which Milton resorts to reinforce his literal meaning. There is a third difference. Unlike Milton's bees, Homer's are quite evidently wild bees; they live in rock clefts, and we are not aware, as they fly from flower patch to flower patch, that theirs is in any sense a patterned or disciplined activity.

By Virgil's time, bees had come to be admired for other reasons; and, when Virgil imitates Homer's simile, it is the ordered, laborious, and constructive modus vivendi of the bees which receives the major emphasis. Virgil likens the Tyrians, Queen Dido's subjects, who are hard at work in diverse portions of the city, digging harbors, building houses, here laying the foundation for a theater, there rearing a citadel (*arx*; cf. Milton's "Straw-built Cittadel"), to bees plying their separate tasks under the early-summer sun.

> qualis apes aestate nova per florea rura
> exercet sub sole labor, cum gentis adultos
> educunt fetus, aut cum liquentia mella
> stipant et dulci distendunt nectare cellas,
> aut onera accipiunt venientum, aut agmine facto
> ignavum fucos pecus a praesepibus arcent;
> fervet opus redolentque thymo fragrantia mella.
>
> 1.430–36

Even as bees when summer is fresh over the flowery country ply their task beneath the sun when they lead forth their nation's grown brood, or when they press the liquid honey and strain their cells with nectarous sweets, or relieve the loaded incomers, or in banded array drive the idle herd of drones far from their folds; the hive is aswarm, and the odorous honey smells sweet of thyme.

Milton's rehandling of Homer's simile has obviously been influenced by the Virgilian imitation. Both the later poets introduce the sun into the comparison, a detail missing from the simile in the *Iliad*. Also Milton's "Pour forth thir populous youth" (1.770) virtually translates Virgil's *gentis adultos / educunt fetus* ("they lead forth their nation's grown brood"). Both poets lend emphasis to their verbs by putting them at the head of their lines. True, Virgil's simile has no auditory function. But if a literary precedent is insisted upon, one may find it easily enough by turning to the Sixth Book of the *Aeneid*. There the voices of the damned hovering about the River Lethe are likened to the murmuring of bees in summer meadows (6.707–9).

Milton's indebtedness to Virgil's fine simile comparing the bees

with the Tyrians in the act of building Carthage should have a special interest for us. Coming in the place it does, Milton's bee simile
heavily underscores the structural parallel between the building of
Pandemonium in the First Book of *Paradise Lost* and the building
of Carthage in the First Book of the *Aeneid*.

But, for all this, the most significant influence on Milton's simile
derives neither from the *Iliad* nor the *Aeneid*. It comes from the
famous Fourth Book of Virgil's *Georgics*. This poem is cast in the
form of a mock epic. As the poem informs us, its purpose is to unfold
the "wondrous show of a tiny state" — the kingdom of bees — embellished with a description of its social and domestic structure, its
mores and its works, its politics and its leadership, how it conducts
itself in war and peace. This purpose is the clue to the treatment
which Virgil accords his subject. From first to last, with a grave and
affectionate irony, Virgil cultivates the epic style and manner. What
mighty warriors the bees are! All the heroic virtues — and in good
measure, too — are resident in them. No wonder that their hearts
beat fast when they hear the challenging notes of the war trumpets.
Nevertheless,

> Hi motus animorum atque haec certamina tanta
> pulveris exigui iactu compressa quiescunt.
>   4.86–87

These stormy passions and these mighty conflicts will be lulled to rest by
a handful of scattered dust.

Consistently, throughout the *Fourth Georgic*, Virgil describes the
bees in human terms. Verbal parallels make it certain that Milton
had at least part of this description in mind. At eventide, says Virgil,
the bees, wearied with the labors of the day, return to their hives,
where after refreshing their bodies (or as Milton has it, "New rub'd
with Baum"), they hum around the edges of the doorway (*mussant-
que oras et limina circum*) before they enter their cells for the night
(4.185–90). So "on the smoothed Plank / The suburb of thir Straw-
built Cittadel," do Milton's bees "confer / Thir State affairs" until
they are "straitn'd" and the Council begins.

Clearly we are meant to recall the *Fourth Georgic* when we encounter Milton's bee simile. Milton compares the Fallen Angels with
a swarm of bees. Now these same angels had been previously linked —
and not merely once but several times — with the insurgent mythological giants who sought to overthrow the Olympians. It is, therefore, of more than passing interest that one of the similes in the
Fourth Georgic should involve a satirical comparison between the

bees and the Cyclops, the impious giants who (in the version of the legend Virgil followed) were punished by being compelled to do slave labor in the boiling furnaces below Mount Etna.[13]

The purpose of Virgil's simile is to illustrate the division of labor among the bees. The Cyclops are specialists; each has his special task to perform. Now, as Milton's editors have remarked, the hill to which the Fallen Angels repair to dig out the materials for the building of Pandemonium bears a certain resemblance to Mount Etna, as Virgil had described it.[14]

> There stood a Hill not far whose griesly top
> Belch'd fire and rowling smoak; the rest entire
> Shon with a glossie scurff, undoubted sign
> That in his womb was hid metallic Ore,
> The work of Sulphur.
>
> 1.670–74

The analogy, however, does not stop at this point. The Fallen Angels, like the Cyclops and the bees, are specialists; one group, under the expert direction of Mammon, mines the metallic ore; another group melts it; a third builds the forms into which the molten metal is poured. This threefold division of labor is too much like that of the other ironworkers to be accidental. The bee simile opens out into one more oblique allusion to the giants who warred on Jove.

The *Fourth Georgic*, which contributed so much to the development of Milton's simile, also helps to define its meaning. Until the bee simile occurs, the Fallen Angels have had pretty much the best of it. We have listened to the majestic, thunderous speeches of their leaders and have been impressed. We have watched them respond with alacrity, and out of a genuine loyalty and courage, to the inspiring words of Satan, and we have been impressed. We have witnessed the miraculous building of Pandemonium, and that too was impressive. Confronted by this awesome display of heroic energy, the unreflective reader may succumb to the fallacy of seeing the Fallen Angels as they see themselves.

Elsewhere Milton has dealt with this danger by interpolating reassuring moral comments *in propria persona*, as when, after Satan has extricated himself from the Burning Lake, Milton reminds the

---

[13] See 4.170–78: "And even as when the Cyclopean forgers of the thunder hurry on the ductile ore, some make the wind come and go in bellows of bull-hide, some dip the hissing brass in the trough; Etna groans under their anvils' pressure, as alternating they lift their arms mightily in time, and turn the iron about in the grip of their tongs: even so, if small things may be compared with great, are our Attic bees urged on each in her proper duty by inborn love of possession."

[14] *Aen.* 3.570–77. The passage is quoted and discussed above, pp. 60–61.

reader that he could never have done so without God's permission. The bee simile does the same work in far less obtrusive fashion. Any tendency the reader may have had to exaggerate the importance of the heroic virtues displayed by the Fallen Angels should be sternly checked by the sobering reflection that Virgil's bees exhibit the same virtues. They too are valorous in battle, resolute in defeat, and fanatically loyal to their leader. In addition, they were celebrated for their skill in building and architecture.

The influence of the *Fourth Georgic* also crystallizes more clearly the situation of the Fallen Angels in the total scheme of Milton's universe. For all their energy, they are as helpless before God as Virgil's bees are at the mercy of their keeper. We know that God has only to stretch forth his hand and all this heroic activity will cease. Or, as Gabriel had informed Satan, God

> . . . with solitarie hand
> Reaching beyond all limit at one blow
> Unaided could have finisht thee, and whelm'd
> Thy Legions under darkness;
>
> 6.139–42

From what has been said so far, it must be clear to every reader that by far the most significant classical influence on *Paradise Lost* is the *Aeneid* of Virgil. Homer figures largely too; but perhaps mainly as a result of the relatively feeble status of Greek in Milton's England, less obviously. Milton's allusions to the Homeric story are either overt, and hence easy to recognize, or so vague and general that one cannot be really sure that they are allusions. Furthermore, as we have seen, the situation is complicated by the fact that a good deal of the Homeric influence is filtered down through the *Aeneid*.

The one large exception is Milton's description of the War in Heaven. Even Virgil's most aggressive admirers have always conceded that Homer had no peer when it came to depicting battles, and the War in Heaven furnishes proof enough that Milton must have shared the prevalent view. Homer, and to a lesser extent Hesiod, here become his chief models, and the influence of the *Aeneid* temporarily wanes. Elsewhere in *Paradise Lost*, and quite consistent with Milton's treatment of the War in Heaven, direct allusions to the *Iliad* are most likely to occur whenever he is describing individual warriors, or bodies of them, in warlike actions or attitudes. Indeed, the very first martial movement the Fallen Angels execute in Hell contains a reminiscence of the opening lines of the *Third Iliad*.

Now when they were arrayed, each company with their captains, the Trojans marched with clamour and with shouting like unto birds, even as when there goeth up before heaven a clamour of cranes which flee from the coming of winter and sudden rain, and fly with clamour towards the streams of ocean, bearing slaughter and fate to the Pigmy men, and in early morn offer cruel battle. But on the other side marched the Achaians in silence breathing courage, eager at heart to give succour to man [p. 45].

In just such a fashion the Fallen Angels are marshaled into ranks and march forward, "Breathing united force with fixed thought" (1.559–61). And Satan's heart distends with pride,

> . . . For never since created man
> Met such imbodied force, as nam'd with these
> Could merit more then that small infantry
> Warr'd on by Cranes:
>
> 1.573–76

With the mention of the warfare between the cranes and the pygmies, coming in such proximity to the earlier passage, the allusion would appear to be confirmed.

It is not always so easy, however, to detect Milton's verbal adaptations of Homer. Often a passage in *Paradise Lost* may simply have an intangible Homeric quality about it, something which no amount of analysis can bring to the surface. In such cases, the baffled critic has little recourse except to fall back on Newton's sensible position. Of those portions of the War in Heaven which have the Homeric ring but which contain no perceptible Homeric echoes, Newton observes rather dejectedly: "One may see plainly that he has read him, even where he does not imitate him." [15]

What has been said of the borrowings from Homer applies, with equal force, to Milton's borrowings from the Athenian dramatists. We know from his constant references to them that Milton had read widely in their works. We know that he owned a copy of the plays of Euripides, which he annotated liberally in the spirit of true scholarship. We know the high regard for these dramatists he expressed in the critical observations he prefixed to his own great play on the classical model, *Samson Agonistes*. Lastly, there is the play itself — *Samson Agonistes* — convincing evidence of his intimate knowledge of their art. Under such circumstances, it would be normal to expect that the influence of the Athenian dramatists would be pervasive at all levels. But it is not. True, the notes of the editors, particularly those of Todd, frequently refer the reader to parallels in Greek dramatic literature. But relatively few of these parallels are close

---

[15] See the note to *P.L.* 6.239.

enough to enable a student of them to contend, with honest assurance, that an influence is present. The main reason for this state of affairs is not far to seek. If Milton could not depend on his readers for a close verbal knowledge of Homer, he could depend even less upon their familiarity with the text of a Greek play.

There may be another reason why the influence of the Greek tragedies is such a shadowy one. Milton, we know, distinguished very carefully between the different poetic genres. Throughout his life, the chief influences on a given poem were always exerted by poets who had written in the same genre to which that poem belonged. In the light elegies written at Cambridge, for example, Ovid had been Milton's master because Ovid had the reputation of being the most skilled practitioner in that kind of poetic composition. So it may be that Milton deliberately sought to exclude extraepical influences from his poem or at least tried to keep them muted. If we except the Bible and sources related to it, the fact remains that only the authors of epics have made major contributions to *Paradise Lost*. Borrowings from poems in other genres are comparatively few and usually unimportant in nature. In other words, Milton's respect for the purity of the genre may help to account for the exceedingly minor role the Athenian dramatists seem to have played in the writing of *Paradise Lost*. It would also explain why Spenser's *Faerie Queene* had more influence on the poem than all of Shakespeare's plays put together.

Unquestionably Milton had learned a good deal from the Greek tragedians, and undoubtedly in subtle, intangible ways they have influenced the composition of *Paradise Lost*. But on the surface they are not a force to be reckoned with. If the plays of Aeschylus, Sophocles, and Euripides had never been written, there is no assurance that *Paradise Lost* would have been markedly different from what it is today.

In every borrowing from classical literature, Milton was guided by one inviolable principle. This was the great Renaissance principle of decorum, always for Milton "the grand masterpiece to observe." He never forgot that he was writing a Christian poem on a Christian theme. To have made any principal use of the substance of classical literature would, in his view, have been a violation of aesthetic propriety. Half a century ago, Charles G. Osgood, after a careful study of Milton's mythological allusions in the English poems, came to the conclusion that "Frequently as they occur it is impossible to find one of them which is not in some way subordinate to a ruling

idea or truth." [16] The statement may safely be extended to include
all of Milton's uses of classical literature.

Milton borrowed descriptive details from the classical poets whenever he could assimilate them without changing or distorting in any
way the fundamental meaning of the scriptural passage he was illustrating. So careful was he in this respect that he made it a practice,
whenever he could, to borrow from concepts or myths which had at
least a quasi-biblical authority. Such, for example, was the myth
of the War between the Giants and the Gods, which tradition held to
be a pagan adaptation of the War of the Angels implied in the Bible.
Whether Milton actually believed this or not is a matter of no great
moment. But no one will gainsay that the flourishing tradition be-
stowed an added propriety upon Milton's systematic exploitation
of the idea in his delineation of the Fallen Angels. The same point
may be made with respect to Milton's description of the Creation,
both macrocosm and microcosm, and of the Universal Flood. As I
have tried to show in an earlier study, he felt justified in filling out
the unadorned accounts of these events in Genesis from their analogues in the *Metamorphoses* because of the intrenched belief that
Ovid's descriptions were actually based upon Genesis.[17] Milton's version of the Creation of Man provides a good example of the way he
habitually worked.

"And God said, Let us make man in our image after our likeness: and let them have dominion over the fish of the sea, and over
the fowl of the air, and over the cattle, and over all the earth, and
over every creeping thing that creepeth upon the earth" (1.26). So
runs the bare account in Genesis. In translating this passage into
blank verse, Milton followed his invariable practice; that is, he
stayed as close to the actual text of the Bible as the exigencies of his
meter permitted (7.519–23). But Milton's account of the Creation
of Man begins with a passage for which there is no biblical authority
whatsoever.

> There wanted yet the Master work, the end
> Of all yet don; a Creature who not prone
> And Brute as other Creatures, but endu'd
> With Sanctitie of Reason, might erect
> His Stature, and upright with Front serene
> Govern the rest, self-knowing, and from thence
> Magnanimous to correspond with Heav'n,
> But grateful to acknowledge whence his good

[16] *The Classical Mythology of Milton's English Poems* (New York, 1900), p. xlv.
[17] Harding, pp. 67–85.

> Descends, thither with heart and voice and eyes
> Directed in Devotion, to adore
> And worship God Supream, who made him chief
> Of all his works:
>
> 7.505–16

The notion that God endowed Man with a higher rational faculty to distinguish him from the animals is not biblical. Nor is the idea that Man was created upright to the end that he might direct his gaze toward Heaven in worshipful devotion. These concepts in the process of time had sifted their way into the Christian theological tradition, but the Bible does not specifically establish them. By a coincidence judged too remarkable to be accidental, however, Ovid in his *Metamorphoses* includes both concepts in his description of the making of Man.

> Sanctius hic animal mentisque capacius altae
> deerat adhuc et quod dominari in cetera posset:
> natus homo est, sive hunc divino semine fecit
> ille opifex rerum, mundi melioris origo,
> sive recens tellus seductaque nuper ab alto
> aethere cognati retinebat semina caeli.
> quam satus Iapeto, mixtam pluvialibus undis,
> finxit in effigiem moderantum cuncta deorum,
> pronaque cum spectent animalia cetera terram,
> os homini sublime dedit caelumque videre
> iussit et erectos ad sidera tollere vultus:
>
> 1.76–86

A living creature of finer stuff than these, more capable of lofty thought, one who could have dominion over all the rest, was lacking yet. Then man was born: whether the god who made all else, designing a more perfect world, made man of his own divine substance, or whether the new earth, but lately drawn away from heavenly ether, retained still some elements of its kindred sky — that earth which the son of Iapetus mixed with fresh, running water, and moulded into the form of the all-controlling gods. And, though all other animals are prone, and fix their gaze upon the earth, he gave to man an uplifted face and bade him stand erect and turn his eyes to heaven.

Upon this passage the Church Fathers, notably the so-called Christian Cicero, Lactantius, had conferred an authority almost equal to that of Holy Writ itself. For the purposes of poetry, at any rate, this was all the authority that Milton needed. Verbal parallels too obvious to enumerate confirm the borrowing.

A final word. No matter where we are in the poem, we are always conscious that it is Milton, and no other poet, who is addressing us. The same tremendous rhythmic impulses inform the speeches of God, Satan, and Adam. Yet the texture of these speeches is so different that it is easily possible to distinguish between three main kinds of style — the styles of Hell, of Paradise, and of Heaven. Here, too, the principle of balance and contrast characteristic of the architecture of the poem as a whole operates to clarify its outlines and enforce its meanings. The concrete style of Hell is balanced against the abstract style of Heaven. In between is the style of Paradise, a mixture of the concrete and the abstract. Unfallen Adam and Eve speak with the tongues of angels but it is against the background of the lush Garden. There is even a detectable movement of the language toward more and more concreteness as the actual moment of the Fall draws nearer. The account of the Fall itself is as concrete as anything in the first two books. Then, appropriately, with the beginning of the reconcilement between Adam and Eve, the pendulum starts swinging again in the other direction. This shift in direction is emphasized by the vividly concrete descriptions which directly precede it: the metamorphosis of the Fallen Angels into serpents, the arrival of the "Hellish pair," Sin and Death, in Paradise, and the disorder introduced into Nature by the Fall.

We should expect these general tendencies to affect the distribution of classical "ornament" throughout the poem, and they do. The books which are most highly colored by classical influences are the first two, the fourth, the ninth, and now and then the tenth. In other words, these influences are always strongest when we are in the felt presence of Evil. The Sixth Book illustrates the method in miniature. The classical allusions which abound in the actual description of the War in Heaven drop out altogether with the victory of the forces of Good. B. Rajan has gone to the trouble of assembling statistics, and his findings require no further comment. "According to my count," he says, "2140 lines of *Paradise Lost* are set in Heaven. Yet in all these lines there is not a single complex or multiple simile, only one simile which involves a literary allusion, and only one place name, Biblical or classical." [18]

A discrepancy so marked can hardly be accidental. The conclusion is inescapable that the way in which Milton has deployed his classical allusions was part of his master plan, enforcing the fundamental contrast between Good and Evil, and at the same time providing the forces of the latter with the kind of poetical stature they must have to preserve, in the minds of fallen readers, the hazy mirage of equality.

---

[18] *Paradise Lost and the 17th Century Reader* (London, 1947), pp. 163–64, note 26.

CHAPTER SIX

Answerable Style

The modern reader of *Paradise Lost* is likely to give short shrift to its brief preface — if indeed he does not ignore it entirely. It seems inevitable now that Milton should have written his poem in blank verse. But it was far from being inevitable then. The preface, in fact, records what was perhaps for Milton the most important artistic decision of his life, a decision affecting not only the poem itself in every detail of its composition but the whole subsequent history of English poetry.

With typical straightforwardness, Milton comes to the point at once. "The Measure is *English* Heroic Verse without Rime, as that of *Homer* in *Greek* and of *Virgil* in *Latin*." He goes on to condemn the use of rhyme "in longer Works especially" as "the Invention of a barbarous Age, to set off wretched matter and lame Meeter" and laments its popularity at the present time. Since rhyme hobbles a poet unnecessarily, it has not been "without cause" that certain "*Italian* and *Spanish* Poets of prime note have rejected Rime both in longer and shorter Works, as have also long since our best *English* Tragedies. . . . " The "true musical delight" derives from other sources, principally from "apt Numbers, fit quantity of Syllables, and the sense variously drawn out from one Verse into another. . . . " Finally, he lays claim to the distinction of having provided, in *Paradise Lost*, a concrete example, "the first in *English*, of ancient liberty recover'd to Heroic Poem from the troublesom and modern bondage of Rimeing." [1] The full importance of this gallant little manifesto cannot be appreciated outside its historical context.

To begin with, the statement that *Paradise Lost* was the first English epic to be written in rhymeless verse is literally true. In the 1540's, Henry Howard, the Earl of Surrey, who is generally credited with having introduced blank verse into England, had adopted the measure for his translation of the Second and Fourth Books of the *Aeneid*,

---

[1] "The Verse." I quote from Vol. III (pp. 71–72) of *John Milton's Complete Poetical Works*, cited earlier.

but the priority of this work obviously does not invalidate Milton's claim. Milton was not thinking of translations but of original poetry. Between Surrey's time and Milton's, there had been a few experiments in nondramatic blank verse, but nothing had been produced of truly epic stature. In England, at least, blank verse remained virtually the exclusive property of the dramatists.[2]

The revolutionary character of Milton's preface would therefore not have been lost upon his contemporaries. They would scarcely have applauded him for it. The tide, as Milton acknowledges, was running too strongly in the other direction. Everywhere rhyme was in vogue. In 1650 Davenant had published his epic *Gondibert* and, in a dedicatory preface to Hobbes, had stoutly defended the heroic quatrains in which it was written. More important, in view of the latter's contemporary influence, was Hobbes's reply, published in the same volume. This reply was full of high praise for Davenant's achievement and undoubtedly tended to diminish any disposition there might have been at the time to evaluate that jejune poem fairly and objectively. Then, in 1677, appeared Dryden's epic in miniature, *Annus Mirabilis*, also in heroic quatrains, followed, in the next year, by Cowley's *Davideis*, composed in couplets. Finally, rhyme even invaded that last stronghold of blank verse, the playhouse, and there too carried the day.[3] At such a time, in the 1660's and 1670's, the only way for Milton to gain supporters for his view was to win them by demonstration; the critics who would have been warmly receptive from the beginning — Ascham, Puttenham, Sidney, Webbe, Campion — were all in their graves.

But the demonstration did not quite win over John Dryden. "Neither will I justify Milton for his blank verse," he tells his readers, and then somewhat patronizingly adds, "though I may excuse him, by the example of Hannibal Caro, and other Italians, who have used

---

[2] As Milton indicates in the preface, the situation was somewhat different on the Continent. Both in Spain and Italy, sporadic attempts had been made to employ blank verse in the service of nondramatic poetry. Of Italian works in the so-called *versi sciolti*, the best known perhaps are Trissino's *Italia Liberata* (1548), Alamanni's *La Cultivazione* (1546), and Tasso's poem on the Creation, *Le Sette Giornata* (1592). Boscan's *Historia de Leandro y Hero* (1543), Gonzalo Perez's incomplete translation of the *Odyssey* (1552), and Figueroa's *Tirzi* (1625) are examples of Spanish poems written in the measure. The dates are those of publication. With the one possible exception of Tasso's poem, it is inconceivable that any of these works materially influenced Milton in his choice of a meter for *Paradise Lost*. Uninspired and tedious, if they proved anything at all, it was that blank verse was not a satisfactory vehicle for epic poetry.

[3] Possibly Milton's remark in the preface that the "best" English tragedies had rejected rhyme was aimed at Dryden, who, in the *Essay of Dramatic Poesy* (1668), had said that the rhymed couplet was the ideal metrical form for drama.

it." [4] The real reason why Milton rejected rhyme as a vehicle for *Paradise Lost*, he alleges, was that "rhyme was not his talent" — and cites the evidence of the *juvenilia* (II, 30). This is surely to do Milton an injustice. As the preface ought to prove, the decision to use blank verse reflected primarily an aesthetic, not a personal, compulsion. Nothing else would have fitted in with his plans. And Dryden, who had wrestled with the same problem, should have known better.

Dryden's translation of the *Aeneid* in couplets (1696) is considered by some scholars and critics to be the finest verse translation of that poem in the English language. But Dryden was too good a poet and Latinist, and too humble a disciple of his master Virgil, to be arrogant in making special claims for his medium. On the contrary, near the end of the valuable essay which prefaces his translation, he confesses that "the French and Italians, as well as we, are yet ignorant what feet are to be used in Heroic Poetry" (II, 218). Knowing the unqualified admiration which all Renaissance critics shared for the Latin hexameter, we may safely surmise that there would have been no problem if that measure could have been domesticated. But it could not; the experiment, conducted along both quantitative and accentual lines, had been tried during the reigns of Elizabeth and James and, except for a few isolated lyrics, the results had been lamentable. So seventeenth-century poets faced up to the facts, reluctantly abandoned the project, and devoted their energies to searching diligently for the English verse form which most nearly approximated the classical hexameter. That is, they began seeking a measure at once both dignified enough and flexible enough to recapture in English something not unlike the effects of style which Virgil had so beautifully exemplified for them in the Latin language.

The prime prerequisite for such a style was loftiness. Here, again, we encounter the Renaissance idea of the genre and its corollary, the principle of decorum. The more noble the theme and subject matter of a poem, the more its style should aim at a corresponding nobility. As the acknowledged "king" of the genres, the epic theoretically demanded the loftiest expression of which the language was capable. But in what did loftiness consist? From Vida to Addison, neoclassical critics were in total agreement. A style is elevated in proportion to its remoteness from everyday speech.[5] As to the specific means by

---

[4] *Essays*, II, 29. All references to Dryden's prose are to the edition of Ker, cited earlier.

[5] This doctrine, which the earlier critics doubtless got from Quintilian, ultimately derives from Aristotle (see his *Poetics*, no. 22). The latter, however, does not supply a very full bill of particulars, specifying only three principal methods

which this loftiness was to be produced, however, the critics remain largely silent. Instead, they implore the fledgling epic poet to study Virgil.

It is really quite astonishing, in view of Virgil's status as a model during the Middle Ages and Renaissance, that no critic before Tasso took it upon himself to analyze the individualizing qualities of his style, the qualities which made it distinctively "Virgilian." This did not come until the vernaculars in Italy, France, and England had supplanted Latin as the literary language. Imitative poets were then obliged to change their strategy. It is one thing to imitate a poet in his own language, a far different thing to imitate him in another. Translators staggered under the heaviest burden. To distill in a vernacular language as much as possible of the "spirit" of one of the great classical poets was as honorable a task as a Renaissance poet could aspire to; but, as the attempts multiplied and likewise the failures, translators became more and more querulous. It is possible to trace a growing decrease in confidence from the first enthusiastic attempts at translation in the fifteenth century to the apologetic prefaces of late seventeenth-century translations. The translators of the *Aeneid* were especially vulnerable to fits of frustration. The truth was that they had gradually become acutely conscious of linguistic differences so basic that no ordinary means would serve to overcome them. It was a bitter pill to swallow.

The problem is as insoluble today as it ever was. Only a few years ago one of the most distinguished of living English poets tried his hand at a verse translation of the *Aeneid*. In his foreword, C. Day Lewis warns readers not to expect too much. He has done his level best but, as he rather wistfully observes, "to find an equivalent for Virgil's language, his choice and arrangement of words — this can hardly be done." Nor is it possible to reproduce "the melodic variety and the complexity of rhythm" which Virgil had wrested from the hexameter. English has too many monosyllables, and so on.[6] These are the old complaints. The first Englishman to document fully his anguish on the subject was John Dryden. He is also the first Englishman to make and publish a careful study of Virgil's style. What he

---

by which an epic style might be raised above the commonplace: by the use of "strange" (that is, alien) words and phrases, by the use of metaphor, and by the arbitrary lengthening, contraction, and alteration of words. The third method, of course, would find its best application in the Greek language. Words in other languages, including Latin, are much less susceptible to the kind of manipulation Aristotle recommends.

[6] *The Aeneid of Virgil* (London, 1952).

has to say will throw a powerful, if indirect, light on the reasons which led Milton to adopt the metrical principles he champions in his preface.

In a letter to Dennis, published by the latter in 1696 but written perhaps as early as March, 1694, Dryden says flatly: "If I undertake the translation of Virgil, the little I can perform will shew at least that no man is fit to write after him in a barbarous modern tongue." [7] Apparently the actual work of translation did much to fortify that conviction. Time after time, in his dedicatory essay, Dryden finds cause to stress the relative inferiority of the English language to the Latin as a vehicle for poetry. Thus, after disclosing that each succeeding book of the *Aeneid* gave him more difficulty than its predecessor, he provides the following explanation: "For Virgil, above all poets, had a stock, which I may call almost inexhaustible, of figurative, elegant, and sounding words: I, who inherit but a small portion of his genius, and write in a language so much inferior to the Latin, have found it very painful to vary phrases, when the same sense returns upon me. . . . Virgil called upon me in every line for some new word; and I paid so long that I was almost bankrupt" (II, 231–32). If Virgil's dignity of expression, which elsewhere Dryden had termed his "chief ornament" (II, 18), was impossible to rival in English, so was the famed Virgilian conciseness. "He studies brevity more than any other poet," says Dryden and then adds, "but he had the advantage of a language wherein much may be comprehended in a little space" (II, 227). And Dryden deplores the plethora of "articles and pronouns, besides signs of tenses and cases, and other barbarities" which clutter up the English language and for which he blames "our forefathers" (II, 227).

His gravest misgivings, however, were reserved for the relative poverty of the sounds of English words. Here I must quote him at some length.

There is a beauty of sound, as Segrais has observed, in some Latin words, which is wholly lost in any modern language. He instances in that *mollis amaracus*, on which Venus lays Cupid, in the *First Aeneid*. If I should translate it *sweet marjoram*, as the word signifies, the reader would think I had mistaken Virgil: for those village words, as I may call them, give us a mean idea of the thing; but the sound of the Latin is so much more pleasing, by the just mixture of the vowels with the consonants, that it raises our fancies to conceive somewhat more noble than a common herb, and to spread roses under him, and strew lilies over him; a bed not unworthy the grandson of the goddess [II, 233].

---

[7] Letter XI in Scott's *Dryden*, Vol. XVIII. Quoted by Ker, *Essays*, II, 279.

A veteran contemporary translator, the late Professor Gilbert Murray, takes a similar view. Contrasting a passage from Keats with one from Pope, Murray notes of the former: "In mere variety and richness of sound this is much nearer to the classical models, though I think one must never expect from the English language a sonority like that of Greek and Latin." [8] In fact, in Murray's opinion, it is precisely Dryden's failure to recapture in English Virgil's authentic music which constitutes his greatest failure. "If one asks why Dryden's translation of Vergil is so utterly unsatisfying, it is partly, no doubt, because Dryden is apt to miss or coarsen the delicate poetry of his original, but even more it is that he substitutes for a deep and sonorous music a sort of thin, impetuous rattle of sound." [9] Cruel words indeed, especially in the light of Dryden's clear-eyed recognition of the lions in his path and his claim to have reached at least a partial solution. "I have endeavoured to make Virgil speak such English as he would himself have spoken, if he had been born in England, and in this present age" (II, 228).

In common with most other poets of his day, Dryden believed that loftiness of expression was a matter of sound as well as of elegance. Imitative harmony with them was a desirable and attainable goal; that is, by means of "sound" they were constantly seeking to reproduce physical sensations. But these were incidental effects. The main job of an epic poet was to maintain, from first to last, a high level of what Dryden calls "sounding words." Words should be resonant; they should have a good, round, mouth-filling quality. Nor should the poet fail to take into account the factor of sound in the ordering of words. Thus, Dryden commends Virgil because he "is everywhere elegant, sweet, and flowing in his hexameters. His words are not only chosen, but the places in which he ranks them for the sound. He who removes them from the station wherein their master set them, spoils the harmony. What he says of the Sibyl's prophecies may be as properly applied to every word of his: they must be read in order as they lie; the least breath discomposes them; and somewhat of their divinity is lost" (II, 215). But here, likewise, the English translator is plagued with difficulties not of his own making. Dryden complains that it is impossible to achieve the polysyllabic fluidity of Virgil's hexameters in a language made up predominantly of heavy monosyllables. In fact, even the structure of English words works against fluidity, he goes on to say, since in English the propor-

---

[8] *The Classical Tradition in Poetry* (Cambridge, Mass., 1927), p. 101.
[9] Murray, p. 100.

tion of vowels to consonants is much less than it is in Latin, where Dryden claims a near balance is struck.[10]

What, then, is the translator to do? How is he to meet the challenge? On one point Dryden is very clear. The translator should do everything within his power to eliminate as much of the native English roughness from his verse as possible. His problem, in a sense, was just the reverse of Virgil's. Virgil, says Dryden, "judged the vowels to have somewhat of an over-balance, and therefore tempers their sweetness with *caesuras*. Such difference there is in tongues, that the same figure, which roughens one, gives majesty to another" (II, 215). Accordingly, Dryden says that he has followed a deliberate policy in his translation of avoiding caesuras "as much as possibly I could" (II, 215). As another step in the elimination of roughness, he recommends the careful and judicious management of such vowels "as we have" and a close study of their effects, both by themselves and in context. The poet "must also know the nature of the vowels, which are more sonorous, and which more soft and sweet, and so dispose them as his present occasions require: all which, and a thousand secrets of versification beside, he may learn from Virgil, if he will take him for his guide" (II, 216).

It is time now to illustrate Dryden's remarks by comparing a specimen of his translation with the original. I have selected, more or less at random, the following passage from the First Book of the *Aeneid*.

> At pius Aeneas per noctem plurima volvens,
> ut primum lux alma data est, exire locosque
> explorare novos, quas vento accesserit oras,
> qui teneant, nam inculta videt, hominesne feraene,
> quaerere constituit sociisque exacta referre.
> classem in convexo nemorum sub rupe cavata
> arboribus clausam circum atque horrentibus umbris
> occulit; ipse uno graditur comitatus Achate
> bina manu lato crispans hastilia ferro.
>
> 1.305–13

But good Aeneas, nightlong revolving many and many a thing, issues forth, so soon as bountiful light is given, to explore the strange country; to what coasts the wind has borne him, who are their habitants, men or wild beasts, for all he sees is wilderness, this he resolves to search, and bring back the certainty to his comrades. The fleet he hides close in embosoming groves beneath a caverned rock, amid rustling shadow of the woodland; himself,

---

[10] According to Professor A. M. Clark, the proportions are as follows: English 42.4 vowels to 57.6 consonants; Latin 45.7 vowels to 54.3 consonants. Greek, on the other hand, shows a preponderance of vowels over consonants: 54.4 vowels to 45.6 consonants. See Clark's *Studies in Literary Modes* (Edinburgh and London, 1946, pp. 144–45.

Achates alone following, he strides forward, clenching in his hand two broad-headed spears.

Dryden translates:

> Mean time, in shades of night, Aeneas lies:
> Care seized his soul, and sleep forsook his eyes.
> But, when the sun restored the cheerful day,
> He rose, the coast and country to survey,
> Anxious and eager to discover more —
> It looked a wild uncultivated shore:
> But, whether humankind, or beasts alone,
> Possessed the new-found region, was unknown.
> Beneath a ledge of rocks his fleet he hides:
> Tall trees surround the mountain's shady sides:
> The bending brow above a safe retreat provides.
> Armed with two pointed darts, he leaves his friends,
> And true Achates on his steps attends.[11]

It will be conceded at once, I think, that all or most of the points that Dryden made about the linguistic difficulties of translating Virgil into English are here tellingly exemplified. One does not need to be an expert in the Latin tongue to see that the passage from Virgil has a fullness of sound and movement, and an economy of expression, which is missing in the translation. But then, how could the monosyllable "trees," for example, seem otherwise than phonetically pallid beside the rich vowel sounds of the ablative *arboribus* or the alliterated phrase "shady sides" hope to achieve the majestic roll of *horrentibus umbris*? Everyone will acknowledge that Dryden was right. The English language simply does not have the resources.

But there is also perhaps another sense in which English — at least Dryden's English — was not up to it. Let us look again at the passage from the *Aeneid*. It will be noticed that the rhythmical movement initiated in the first line carries through to the end of the fifth. In terms of structure, the rhythm is cumulative and crescendo-like, rising clause by clause, until the main verb *constituit* is reached; then, and not until then, is the full meaning of the preceding lines released. The next rhythmical impulse is of the same character, subsiding with the main verb *occulit*, in the penultimate line. Technically, it differs from the preceding movement merely in that it is smooth enough to require no internal punctuation. Both movements exemplify the tendency toward periodic structure — a distinguishing feature of the Virgilian style. But it is Virgil's pioneer development and exploitation of the verse paragraph which most markedly sets

---

[11] *The Works of John Dryden*, ed. Sir Walter Scott and G. Saintsbury (Edinburgh, 1889), Vol. XIV, lines 420–32.

him off from other poets. Before Virgil and contemporaneous with him, the rhythmical unit had been the single line; with Virgil, however, it is a whole block of lines. The blocks, of course, are of varying lengths and pauses may come anywhere. This fact is important. We are not reading Virgil properly or, what is less likely, Virgil has failed us if we do not feel that each word, phrase, clause, or line is a working part of the larger whole which is the verse paragraph. To order a plethora of syntactical units into a pattern at once both harmonious and meaningful obviously required an extremely flexible language and an ear of unusual delicacy. Latin had the flexibility and Virgil had the ear, a most happy conjunction of talents. It enabled Virgil to attain an amplitude and variety of musical movement within his rhythmical unit which was to remain unparalled for centuries.

There is nothing of all this in Dryden's translation. On the contrary, the English poet has obviously taken pains to restrict the free movement of his verse. The most compelling restraint is, of course, the heroic couplet. Dryden makes no attempt in the preface to defend his choice of this measure, but one of his reasons, at least, may be gathered from what he has to say there about his occasional use of the alexandrine. "Spenser has also given me the boldness to make use sometimes of his Alexandrine line. . . . It adds a certain majesty to the verse, when it is used with judgment, and *stops the sense from overflowing into another line*" (II, 218; the italics are mine). There is a convenient example of this use of the alexandrine in the quoted passage:

> Beneath a ledge of rocks his fleet he hides:
> Tall trees surround the mountain's shady sides:
> The bending brow above a safe retreat provides.

But how startlingly different the rhythm of these lines is from the corresponding verses in the *Aeneid*! What has happened? We may be sure that as keen a student of Virgil's style as Dryden could not have failed to diagnose his characteristic rhythm. Dryden's abandonment of it must therefore have been deliberate.

Perhaps Dryden realized that English syntax did not have the suppleness or the maneuverability to warrant an attempt to imitate Virgil's complex periods. This would have been a justifiable point of view, but, if Dryden held it, he refrains from explicitly saying so in the preface. On the other hand, he is full of warm praise for Virgilian smoothness and grace, remarking in this connection (the reader will recall) that he had decided to dispense with caesuras whenever possible because they imparted an additional roughness to a language already too much characterized by it. Now strong rests and pauses are hardly to be avoided in poetry, no matter what language it happens to be written in, which is committed to the principle of the verse paragraph. Dryden's dilemma may, therefore, be stated in this way. Without adopting the verse paragraph, he could not hope to imitate Virgil's complex rhythmical movement; and if he did adopt it, he could not hope to imitate Virgil's grace and smoothness — in a word, his majesty. He could have one or the other, but he could not have both. He elected to sacrifice the rhythm.

Now, as I hope to show, this was precisely the sacrifice Milton was not prepared to make. The views of these two great poets were exactly antithetical. Where Dryden was concerned "to stop the sense," Milton was concerned to erect as few barriers as possible to its continuous flow. That is why, we may be reasonably certain, Dryden chose the end-stopped couplet as his instrument and Milton blank verse.

Milton's choice of blank verse was almost as dangerous a gamble as Virgil's selection of the quantitative hexameter. As an epic measure, blank verse had been tested before, though not in English, and Milton must have been only too aware that the backward path was strewn with acknowledged failures. No poet had ever succeeded in raising it to the prescribed loftiness. Two eminent critics, Dr. Johnson in the eighteenth century and T. S. Eliot in the twentieth, have provided at least partial explanations. This is what Dr. Johnson has to say on the subject:

The musick of the English heroick line strikes the ear so faintly that it is easily lost, unless all the syllables of every line co-operate together: this co-operation can be only obtained by the preservation of every verse unmingled with another, as a distinct system of sounds; and this distinctness is obtained and preserved by the artifice of rhyme. The variety of pauses, so much boasted by the lovers of blank verse, changes the measures of an English poet to the periods of a declaimer; and there are only a few skilful and happy readers of Milton, who enable their audience to perceive where the lines end or begin. *Blank verse*, said an ingenious critick, *seems to be verse only to the eye.*[12]

Quoting this passage with approval, Mr. Eliot glances at the blank verse written in the nineteenth century. "Indeed it is only with labour, or by occasional inspiration, or by submission to the influence of the older dramatists, that the blank verse of the *nineteenth* century succeeds in making the absence of rhyme inevitable and right, with

---

[12] "Milton" in *Lives of the English Poets*. Reprinted in *Milton Criticism*, p. 87.

the rightness of Milton." [13] Modern practitioners of blank verse have experienced the same difficulty. Where they "do not touch the sublime," testifies Eliot, "they frequently approach the ridiculous." [14]

This appears to be a fair statement of the case. Let the writer of blank verse relax for a moment his firm control over his medium, and he lapses into prose, usually accompanied by an effect of bathos. And at the other end of the scale there is the ever-present danger of tumidity, what the eighteenth century called the "false sublime." Tumidity and prosiness — these are the Scylla and Charybdis which have always confronted the authors of blank verse. How was Milton to achieve, in a language judged inferior to Greek and Latin, in a measure whose natural tendency was to be earth-bound, a loftiness of utterance comparable to that of Homer and Virgil? We know that Milton regarded his epic subject and theme as the noblest that could be celebrated by the pen of man. But if this gave him an initial advantage over his rival poets, it also increased the burden of his poetic responsibility. Success or failure depended upon his capacity to fashion an "answerable style" — a style, that is, fully as lofty as his subject matter.

It is the principal thesis of this chapter that Milton met the challenge by deliberately forcing the English language to do as much of the work of Latin as it could within reason be made to do.[15] Now this was no mean feat. Like Virgil struggling to adapt Latin words and Latin syntax to an alien prosody,[16] Milton labored under a crushing disadvantage. The great merit of an inflected language like Latin, as compared with an uninflected language like English, is that in the former there is no such thing as a fixed order of words. Declensional and conjugational endings serve to define syntactical relationships and the poet may experiment with any kind of word order he chooses. Thus, he can arrange his ideas and images in the sentence in such a way that they are virtually rated according to the importance he attaches to them. This gives him a greater measure

---

[13] "Milton" (1947). Reprinted in *Milton Criticism*, p. 325.

[14] *Milton Criticism*, pp. 325–26.

[15] But cf. Dryden. This is the main difference between Dryden and Milton. Whereas the former was prepared to make concessions to the relative inadequacies of the English language, Milton was not. Indeed, Milton's attitude toward language was not unlike his attitude toward moral and spiritual delinquency; it was hard, ruthless, and inflexible.

[16] Before Greek cultural influences were felt on the Italian peninsula, the native poetry, such as the so-called *versus Saturnius*, had been strongly accentual in character. The grafting of the Greek quantitative measures on a linguistic stock essentially inimical to them inevitably widened the gulf between the language of poetry and the language of the street.

of control over the responses of his readers. Also, the freedom of Latin word order puts at his disposal a powerful weapon for arousing and stimulating their visual imagination. Let me illustrate with some verses from the specimen passage quoted above.

> classem in convexo nemorum sub rupe cavata
> arboribus clausam circum atque horrentibus umbris
> occulit;
>
> 1.310–12

The fleet he hides close in embosoming groves beneath a caverned rock, amid rustling shadow of the woodland.

The word order indicates that the fact of Aeneas' hiding the ship is not so important to Virgil as the place where he hides it. By withholding the main verb until the very end of the period, he subordinates action to description. Not only does he force us to visualize the scene, he controls the order of our seeing; the eye moves upward, as it were, from the ship in the cove past the overhanging rock to the fringe of trees at the top. By one of those cross references for which Virgil is famous, these lines intimately recall the very first view the shipwrecked Trojans had of the harbor.

> . . . tum silvis scaena coruscis
> desuper horrentique atrum memus imminet umbra;
> fronte sub adversa scopulis pendentibus antrum,
> intus aquae dulces vivoque sedilia saxo,
> nympharum domus.
>
> 1.164–68

Above is a background of waving forest, and a woodland overhangs dark with rustling shade. Beneath the seaward brow is a rock-hung cavern, within it fresh springs and seats in the living stone, a haunt of nymphs.

Together the two passages seem to have been a main inspiration for the verses in which Milton describes Satan's first glimpse of Paradise.

> . . . and over head up grew
> Insuperable highth of loftiest shade,
> Cedar, and Pine, and Firr, and branching Palm,
> A Silvan Scene, and as the ranks ascend
> Shade above shade, a woodie Theatre
> Of stateliest view. Yet higher than thir tops
> The verdurous wall of paradise up sprung:
> Which to our general Sire gave prospect large
> Into his neather Empire and neighbouring round.
> And higher then that Wall a circling row
> Of goodliest Trees loaden with fairest Fruit,
> Blossoms and Fruits at once of golden hue
> Appeerd, with gay enameld colours mixt:
> On which the Sun more glad impress'd his beams

Then in fair Evening Cloud, or humid Bow,
When God hath showrd the earth; so lovely seemd
That Lantskip:

4.137-53

Only the first few verses are perceptibly in Virgil's debt. The phrase "Silvan Scene" (cf. Virgil's *silvis scaena*) is the clue, a typical form of signature which establishes the source of Milton's theater metaphor.[17] The passage as a whole shows plainly why Milton must normally be quoted at length or not at all. The forward impulse of the verse is as irresistible as the movement of a glacier; it must be allowed to exhaust itself. This is Virgil's verse paragraph, but with a difference, for Milton has not only succeeded in achieving Virgil's rhythmic span, he has remarkably extended its limits. For the undeniable loss in grace and serenity, there has been a compensatory gain in rough power. But Dryden, on the implicit evidence of his preface, was clearly right. Virgilian smoothness and the English verse paragraph would indeed appear to be incompatible ideals. Only Spenser had come close to achieving a synthesis. Milton did not even make the attempt.

We observe, further, in the passage from *Paradise Lost* the tendency toward periodic structure so characteristic of Virgil. By holding back his main verbs, "suspending" them as critics have termed the process, Milton like Virgil is able to throw the emphasis where he wants it, in this case on the descriptive details, the garden's "Insuperable highth." The ascending structure here has an obvious relevance. Satan is at the foot of Paradise, and we actually see the Mount as Satan sees it; our eyes follow his upwards. This perspective intensifies our awareness of the awful proximity of Evil to Good and of the crisis in human affairs soon to come. The succeeding verses, as the reader may easily ascertain for himself, continue to work toward the same end — to make us *feel* the physical presence of Satan in the environs of the Garden and ultimately in the Garden itself. Thus, progressively, the tone of gathering and imminent menace deepens.

No English poet has ever strained the bonds of language as Milton strained them. In his valiant effort to obtain something of the advantage of a Latin word order, Milton did not scruple when the need arose to defy the ordinary laws of grammar and syntax. But, as Coleridge saw clearly enough, Milton knew what he was doing; the "logic of passion" was more important to him than the crippling "logic of grammar."

---

[17] The literal meaning of the Latin word *scaena* is the background or scene on the stage of a theater.

The language and versification of the *Paradise Lost* are peculiar in being so much more necessarily correspondent to each other than those in any other poem or poet. The connexion of the sentences and the position of the words are exquisitely artificial; but the position is rather according to the logic of passion or universal logic than to the logic of grammar. Milton attempted to make the English language obey the logic of passion as perfectly as the Greek and Latin. Hence the occasional harshness in the construction.[18]

And recently a modern critic, William Empson, has demonstrated, in example after example, that Milton's "vague or apparently disordered grammar" was not so much an inadvertency as a device for securing complex effects of meaning.[19]

The main difference between Milton's practice and that of the classical poets was that the latter, by having an inflected language for their mother tongue, could achieve their effects without doing a major violence to either grammar or syntax, without risking obscurity. As Professor Naylor has shown in his excellent edition of the *Odes* and *Epodes* of Horace, the Latin poet is able, by a skillful juxtaposition of words and phrases, to bring about an interpenetration of meanings which is simply beyond the reach of a poet writing in English. Thus, one Latin word may often color the meaning of another, although not syntactically related to it; or two phrases in juxtaposition may so influence one another so as to generate a whole set of tangential meanings.[20] Writing in an uninflected language, Milton could not hope to imitate the Roman poets in either the precision or the suppleness of their periods. He could not do the impossible. But by keeping his structures fully as relaxed as his stubborn language would permit, he could imitate many of their effects and at the same time sustain the continuous surging movements so vital to his whole design, "the sense variously drawn out from one Verse into another."

No good purpose, I believe, is served by attempting to minimize the classical influence on the style of *Paradise Lost*. Surely it is illuminating that the impulse to do so, an honorable one, is of fairly recent origin. We no longer have Latin bred into our bones; hence, the admirers of Milton are genuinely troubled lest this deficiency build up a wall between the modern reader and his ability to appreciate the poem. In part, their fears are justified, but it is some consolation to recall that the style of *Paradise Lost* has always been

---

[18] "Milton," Lecture X. Reprinted in *Milton Criticism*, p. 95.

[19] *Some Versions of Pastoral* (London, 1950; first edition, 1935), pp. 161 ff.

[20] H. Darnley Naylor, *Horace: Odes and Epodes, a Study in Poetic Word Order* (Cambridge, Eng., 1922). See the section entitled "Prolegomena," *passim*.

accounted "strange." Dr. Johnson's famous pronouncement will bear requoting: "Through all his greater works there prevails an uniform peculiarity of *Diction*, a mode and cast of expression which bears little resemblance to that of any former writer, and which is so far removed from common use that an unlearned reader, when he first opens the book, finds himself surprised by a new language.[21] But other readers, if Milton's eighteenth-century annotater, Jonathan Richardson, is at all representative, were likely to react quite differently. By having deliberately "Greeked and Latinized" his style, writes Richardson, Milton was able to make it "as uncommon and expressive as our tongue could be, and yet intelligible to us for whom he wrote. But all his images are pure antique, so that we read Homer and Virgil in reading him. We hear them in our own tongue, as we see what they conceived when Milton speaks." And again: "Milton's language is English, but 'tis Milton's English; 'tis Latin, 'tis Greek English; not only the words, the phraseology, the transpositions, but the ancient idiom is seen in all he writes, so that a learned foreigner will think Milton the easiest to be understood of all the English writers." [22]

To suggest the degree of classical influence on Milton's mature style, nothing could be more revealing than his translation of the famed *Fifth Ode* of Horace. No one knows when this translation was written. It was first printed in the 1673 *Poems* and, since it did not appear in the 1645 edition, Mackail conjectures a date of about 1650. The translation is prefaced by the following rubric: "*Quis multa gracilis te puer in Rosa*, Rendred almost word for word without Rhyme according to the Latin Measure, as near as the Language will permit." Here, first of all, is the Latin poem, which I must quote in full.

> Quis multa gracilis te puer in rosa
> Perfusus liquidis urget odoribus,

---

[21] *Milton Criticism*, p. 85. Dr. Johnson's theory that the "foreign" element in the style of *Paradise Lost* is perhaps mainly of Italian origin is the inspiration for one of the best specialized studies of Milton to emerge in recent years, *The Italian Element in Milton's Verse* (Oxford, 1954), by F. T. Prince. As Prince freely acknowledges, however, the influence of the Italians on Milton's style is intermediary; it does not detract from the ultimate debt to Homer and Virgil. "Yet Milton's debt remains of a limited nature; and it should be clear that, however fully it is brought out, it does little to change our idea of Milton's relationship either to his Greek and Roman models or to his English predecessors. Virgil and Homer have always been acknowledged to be Milton's chief mentors. So far from displacing them from this position, an investigation of the Italian element in his verse confirms them in it." Introduction, p. vii.

[22] *Milton Criticism*, pp. 58, 55. Thorpe reprints excerpts from Richardson's *Explanatory Notes and Remarks on Milton's "Paradise Lost,"* published in 1734.

> Grato, *Pyrrha*, sub antro?
> Cui flavam religas comam
> Simplex munditie? heu quotiens fidem
> Mutatosque deos flebit, & aspera
>   Nigris aequora ventis
>   Emarabitur insolens,
> Qui nunc te fruitur credulus aurea:
> Qui semper vacuam, semper amabilem
>   Sperat, nescius aurae
>   Fallacis. miseri quibus
> Intentata nites. me tabula sacer
> Votiva paries indicat uvida
>   Suspendisse potenti
>   Vestimenta maris Deo.[23]

Milton's translation follows:

> What slender Youth bedew'd with liquid odours
> Courts thee on Roses in some pleasant Cave,
>   *Pyrrha* for whom bindst thou
>   In wreaths thy golden Hair,
> Plain in thy neatness; O how oft shall he
> On Faith and changed Gods complain: and Seas
>   Rough with black winds and storms
>   Unwonted shall admire:
> Who now enjoyes thee credulous, all Gold,
> Who alwayes vacant alwayes amiable
>   Hopes thee; of flattering gales
>   Unmindfull. Hapless they
> To whom thou untry'd seem'st fair. Me in my vow'd
> Picture the sacred wall declares t'have hung
>   My dank and dropping weeds
>   To the stern God of Sea.[24]

It will be conceded, I think, that, making allowance for the different verse forms, we have here the genuine Miltonic music, the music of *Paradise Lost*. And this is a literal translation, truly, as Milton says, "word for word." [25] Perhaps a closer look at the poem will help to clarify points I have tried to make in the preceding pages.

---

[23] I follow the Latin text provided by Milton himself (or his publisher), reproduced in Vol. I (p. 46) of the University of Illinois facsimile edition of the *Complete Poetical Works*.

[24] See *Complete Poetical Works*, I, 45, for Milton's translation.

[25] For purposes of comparison, I add Mackail's close prose translation. "What slim boy steeped in liquid scents presses you amid clustered roses, for whom under a pleasant arbour, Fair-hair, you knot back these blonde tresses? Ah, how often shall he weep for faith and gods estranged, and gaze aghast on seas rough with black winds, witless, who now confidingly possesses you, his golden one, who, ignorant of the delusive radiance, expects you always disengaged, always loveable! Luckless they to whom you shine unexplored; me a tablet on the holy wall records to have hung up my dripping garments to the mighty God of the Sea." *Studies*

The poem, which celebrates a joyless victory, is divided into four stanzas. The stanzas interlock — that is, the whole meaning of any one stanza is not confined to it; the words spill over into the next stanza. Thus, the notorious expression *simplex munditie* constitutes what the editors of Horace call an addendum, a phrase or clause which prolongs the rhythmical impulse beyond the reader's expectancy. The technique is even more characteristic of Virgil. In both poets, but especially in Virgil, such addenda vary considerably in length. The communicated effect is that of a force and energy so strong that it resists to the end the efforts of the poet to control and discipline it. In Milton, who imitates — and with magnificent success — this metrical strategy of Horace and Virgil, the tension can become almost unbearable. In the following passage, for example, the rhythmic wave reaches its crest in the middle of the fifth line, with the phrase "Satan exalted sat," but it is another five lines before the momentum of the period has been dissipated.

> High on a Throne of Royal State, which far
> Outshon the wealth of *Ormus* and of *Ind,*
> Or where the gorgeous East with richest hand
> Showrs on her Kings *Barbaric* Pearl and Gold,
> Satan exalted sat, by merit rais'd
> To that bad eminence; and from despair
> Thus high uplifted beyond hope, aspires
> Beyond thus high, insatiate to pursue
> Vain Warr with Heav'n and by success untaught
> His proud imaginations thus displaid.
>
> *P.L.* 2.1–10

Out of many such passages *Paradise Lost* has been made.

One notices, in addition, that the Horatian stanzas do not mark out the organic structure. This structure is based on the three principle movements — or, if one prefers, periods — of the poem. The first movement carries us down to line 5, the second to the middle of line 12, and the third concludes the poem. As he must, of course, in so literal a translation, Milton preserves this basic structure. But we should not underestimate the difficulty of the performance because Milton has made it seem so easy.

We have seen how Dryden resented the little words in English — the articles, prepositions, conjunctions, pronouns, etc. — which made it impossible for him to imitate the brevity of Virgil. Milton has avoided as many of these as he could, but he could not avoid them all. In a word-for-word translation, he still finds it necessary to use

---

in Humanism (London, 1938), p. 68. The translation is included in the course of a detailed analysis of the *Fifth Ode.*

one third again as many words as Horace had used, although he plainly put himself under the most severe kind of restraint. But Latin *brevitas* is not simply a happy linguistic accident. Latin words work harder than English words; their meanings shade off more, ramify more, as any reader can see for himself by consulting a good Latin-English dictionary. A well-known example is the phrase *simplex munditie* (modern editions read *simplex munditiis*). This Milton, disabled by his goal of a literal translation, renders "Plain in thy neatness." The translation is accurate, but no more communicates the complex meaning of *simplex munditie* than Ogilby's pedestrian translation of the *Aeneid* catches the spirit of Virgil. The truth is that the phrase is untranslatable on any literal level; in fact, the wish to capture its full meaning has inspired whole poems.

Milton follows the Latin word order as closely as he dares or, in his own words, "as near as the Language will permit." The reader should compare the position of the verbs in both poems. Except in two instances, the verbs are located in the same lines, indicating the care with which Milton has preserved the periodic structure of his original. In the final movement of the poem, the word order is, in fact, followed so painstakingly that the meaning is partially obscured. Despite the obscurity, the lines are impressive; syntactically they are exactly right and it is this which gives them the strength and beauty inhering in the original. What can happen when Horace's words are accommodated to an English word order may be exemplified by Sir Richard Fanshawe's translation of the same lines.

> For me my Votive Table showes
> That I have hung up my wet Clothes
> Upon the Temple Wall
> Of Seas great Admirall.[26]

And all the poetry has gone out of the passage.

I have already commented upon the way in which an inflected language like Latin is able to juxtapose elements in a sentence so as to condition their meanings. Thus, in lines 5–6 of the *Fifth Ode*, the word *mutatosque* really modifies *deos*, but it is so placed in the sentence that it also colors the meaning of *fidem*. It is not only the gods who are variable and fickle. By a similar device, the word *credulus* in line 9 assumes a double meaning, being applicable to both the young man and the flaxen-haired Pyrrha. The young man is *credulus* in the sense of being naive, readily taken in, an easy victim. But the word is also applicable to the seductive sexuality of

---

[26] *Selected Parts of Horace, Prince of Lyricks* (London, 1652), p. 5.

Pyrrha, hinting at a quality about her which is somehow reminiscent of Eve's "sweet, reluctant, amorous delay." To get both meanings into the word, Milton, as he so often does in *Paradise Lost*, simply transliterates.

Often, however, the language does not have the resources to encourage such freedom. Take the word *insolens* in line 8, for example. Milton, possibly influenced by the punctuation in his copy of Horace, construes the word with what precedes and translates literally, "unwonted." But, from the central position of the word and in the light of the poem's complex meaning, *insolens* may be said to look ahead as well as back. In this case, the word is associated with the rhythmical unit which follows it, taking on its secondary Latin meaning of "arrogant," "insolent" in the pride of possession. The young man is afflicted with a kind of erotic *hybris*, and we are made to feel all the more that his ruin is imminent. But there is no English equivalent for *insolens* which can simultaneously generate both these meanings, and so Milton was obliged to choose between alternatives. The same is true of *aurae* in line 11. On one level, it continues the metaphor of shipwreck and means "breezes" or "gales." The storm is already blowing up which will presumably drown the lover unless he is as fortunate as the *persona* of the poem. On another level, however, the word carries the same signification as our derived word "aura." Mackail, we may note, forgoes the metaphor and renders the word "radiance." Milton translates "gales." Neither apparently could find a way of preserving both meanings.

How well Milton understood this poem may be inferred from a point Mackail makes about its rhythmical structure. Declaring that the punctuation "should follow, not prescribe the phrasing," he deprecates the manner in which modern editions of Horace have defied this principle by putting an interrogation mark after *antro* in line 3 and another after *simplex munditie* in line 4. "But the rhythmical as well as the rhetorical balance seems rather to require the pause to be made at the end of line 2, line 3 running continuously on into line 4. Is *cui* in line 4 a fresh interrogative, or a relative pronoun? Here again the rhythmical structure suggests the latter." [27] Now it is a curious fact that, although the two marks of interrogation Mackail mentions appear in the Latin text of the *Ode* provided in the 1673 edition, they are not reproduced in the translation. Perhaps, as Mackail conjectures, Milton's punctuation reflects his own uncertainty. But it seems more likely that he is following Horace's rhyth-

---

[27] *Studies in Humanism*, p. 68.

mical structure, as he (and Mackail) conceive that structure to be. The point is that Milton's syntax makes it possible for the reader to have it both ways, as Horace's does, if we disregard the arbitrary punctuation of the editors. Here, therefore, we presumably have an instance of that mode of ambiguity which Latin prosody invites and which Milton frequently tried to imitate, in *Paradise Lost*, by a deliberate blurring of syntactical relationships.

For a long time it has been recognized that the rhythmical structures which characterize the verse of *Paradise Lost* were adumbrated in the later sonnets, the sonnets written during the Protectorate. Contrasting the earlier with these later sonnets, the author of the standard edition of the sonnets notes some central differences: "But the sonnets to Cromwell, Vane, and Lawrence, on the Massacre in Piedmont, on his blindness and on the death of his wife are in a different category. In these poems the divisions of the metre and those required by the thought are not brought into strict agreement; pauses occur in any part of the line; and a sentence is sometimes continued, in rapid and unbroken flow, from the second quatrain into the first tercet, the definite pause usually placed after the quatrain being disregarded."[28] By showing that this stylistic development probably reflected the influence of the Italian poet, Della Casa, Professor Smart made an important contribution to Milton studies. But he failed to see, or at least failed to say, that Della Casa's own style was formed from his perceptive study of the styles of Virgil and Horace.[29] Nor does he appear to have taken into any account a fine perception made more than a quarter of a century before his edition appeared. In the course of some critical remarks on the poetry of Keats, Robert Brydges has this to say of Milton's later sonnets:

Again, Horace elaborated a form of ode which is easier to recognize than in few words describe; and a number of Milton's sonnets may be referred to this ode form. If we compare, for example, his *Cyriack, whose grandsire,* with *Martiis caelebs* or *Aeli vetusto*, there can be no doubt that Milton was here deliberately using the sonnet form to do the work of Horace's tight stanzas; and not the whole of Shakespeare's or Petrarch's sonnets set alongside will show enough kinship with these sonnets of Milton to draw them away from their affinity with Horace.[30]

---

[28] John S. Smart, *The Sonnets of Milton* (Glasgow, 1921), p. 27.

[29] For a discussion of Della Casa's style and its influence on Milton, see Prince, pp. 14–33, especially p. 24, where Prince states: "The value of Della Casa's verse to Milton was that it showed him that a modern language could indeed rival the complex word-order of Latin, and gave him many suggestions as to the verbal patterns he could use for this purpose."

[30] *Poems of John Keats*, ed. G. Thorn Drury, with an introduction by Robert Brydges (London, 1894), pp. lxx–lxxi.

Brydges' insight, however, was either overlooked or ignored until, in 1937, an important essay appeared in strong support of his conclusions. [31] If these scholars are right, and the translation of the *Fifth Ode* would seem to be another substantial piece of evidence in their favor, we must certainly suppose that there was a vital connection between Milton's study of the techniques of Horace and Virgil, and the development of his mature epic style.

One need not be reminded of the dangers of trying to isolate the elements of a style formed by the action of external pressures on it from those which are purely personal and individualistic. Working from analogies, which may often be misleading, the student of style can provide at best only tentative conclusions hedged about by uncertainties. But one thing is sure. At no time in the history of English literature could that dubious commonplace, the style is the man, be invoked with less propriety than during the Renaissance. Imitation was the desideratum, and from his earliest days Milton, as we have seen, was an imitative poet. This is a matter of record and strengthens the conviction that, when we find Milton using Virgilian principles to revolutionize English blank verse, the coincidence is not a chance one. *Paradise Lost* remains, when all is said and done, the finest commentary on Virgil's *Aeneid* ever written.

---

[31] John H. Finley, "Milton and Horace," *Harvard Studies in Classical Philology*, XLVIII (1937), 29–73.

Index of Names

Abdiel, 56, 99, 100
Achemenides, 61, 63
Achilles, 13, 25, 27, 31, 32, 33, 35, 44, 46, 47, 48, 50, 51, 66
Addison, Joseph, 116
Aeneas, 27, 28, 29, 30, 31, 38, 44, 48, 49, 50, 51, 58, 65, 70, 71, 87, 88, 96, 98, 99, 100, 101, 103, 125
Aeschylus, 47, 110
Agamemnon, 28, 86, 97, 98
Alamanni, Luigi, 115n
Allecto, 82
Amata, 82
Anchises, 38
Antenor, 28
Apollonius Rhodius, 83
Ariosto, 22
Aristotle, 117n
Ascham, Roger, 18, 115
Asilas, 93
Atreus, 95, 98
Augustus, 38
Avitus, Quintus Octavius, 18

Baldwin, T. W., 3n, 6n
Beelzebub, 46, 92, 93
Belial, 64, 92
Belshazzar, 48
Bennett, C. E., 72n
Blackmore, Richard, 21, 22
Boscan Almogaver, Juan, 115n
Bowra, C. M., 25n, 32, 33, 39, 51n
Briareos, 59
Brinsley, John, 4 ff.
Briseis, 31
Brydges, Robert, 133–34
Butler, Charles, 5n

Caesar, 3
Campion, Thomas, 115
Caro, Hannibal, 115
Carthage, 27

Cato, 3
Chaos, 65
Charybdis, 124
Christ, 38, 41
Chryses, 28
Cicero, 2, 3, 5, 8, 19
Clark, A. M., 120n
Clark, Donald L., 3n, 6n
Clytie, 15
Coleridge, Samuel T., 126
Corderius, 2
Cowley, Abraham, 22, 115
Cyclops, 61, 62, 107

Dalilah, 95
Darbishire, Helen, 6n
Davenant, Sir William, 115
Dawson, Christopher, 2
Death, 64, 94, 113
Della Casa, Giovanni, 133
Demosthenes, 8, 19, 44
Dennis, John, 21, 118
Diana, 88
Dido, 29, 31, 53, 83, 85, 86, 87, 88, 89, 96, 99, 103, 105
Diomedes, 47
Dodge, R. E. Neil, 55n
Dolon, 47
Donatus, 19
Drury, G. Thorn, 133n
Dryden, John, 21, 22, 115, 116–26, 130
Duckworth, George E., 84

E. K., 8
Eliot, T. S., 19, 54n, 70, 93, 123
Elizabeth I, Queen of England, 116
Empson, William, 127
Ennius, 55
Erasmus, 2, 3, 19
Euripides, 3, 8, 109, 110
Eustathius, 71, 100